Encountering North America

ALSO BY THE AUTHORS

We Could Perceive No Sign of Them: Failed Colonies in North America, 1526–1689

Neither Hee Nor Any of His Companie Did Return Againe: Failed Colonies in the Caribbean and Latin America, 1492–1865

Kaskaskia: The Lost Capital of Illinois

Encountering NORTH AMERICA

Profiles of FRONTIERSMEN, 1650-1820

DAVID MACDONALD AND RAINE WATERS

WESTHOLME
Yardley

Westholme Publishing, LLC
904 Edgewood Road
Yardley, Pennsylvania 19067
Visit our Web site at www.westholmepublishing.com

ISBN: 978-1-59416-445-3
Also available as an eBook.

Printed in the United States of America.

David MacDonald
1943–2025

Historian, Numismatist, Linguist,
Professor of ancient Greek & Roman history,
Ancient Chinese Tea enthusiast, Avid Illinois kayaker,
Husband of one wife, Sharon, for sixty years.

To many of us, you were a neighbor, professor,
A wise father figure, teacher, jokester,
Philanthropist of the poor and needy,

But you were simply my beloved friend.
—Raine
"There are companions to keep one company, and
There is a friend more devoted than a brother."
Proverbs 18:24

I put into my operations great activity; I go a great distance while some are considering whether they will start today or tomorrow. —Manuel Lisa

I was in command formerly in these parts for three years; and had not during that time to decide more than one process a week.... At present one is obliged every day to imprison young men who demand that if the English law if favorable to them it should be followed; on another occasion the same people will the very next day demand the old French laws which have always been followed. If I were not a little crazed already, I believe they would cause me to become entirely so.

—Philippe-François de Rastel de Rocheblave

CONTENTS

List of Illustrations *xi*

Introduction *xiii*

1. Prisoner of the Iroquois, Companion of Kings: Pierre-Esprit Radisson 1

2. Rogue, Missouri River Pioneer, Nobleman: Étienne de Véniard de Bourgmont 25

3. Explorer of the South: Jean-Baptiste Bénard, Sieur de la Harpe 37

4. A Family of Explorers: Pierre Gaultier de Varennes et de La Vérendrye and Sons 49

5. Across the Plains to Santa Fe: Pierre Antoine Mallet and Paul Mallet 63

6. Caught Between Two Powers: Jean-Baptiste de Couagne 69

7. Under Three Flags: Philippe-François de Rastel de Rocheblave 73

8. Trader and Patriot:
Daniel-Maurice Godefroy de Linctot 79

9. Promise Unfulfilled:
Joseph L. Bowman 85

10. First Across the Continent:
Alexander Mackenzie 91

11. Frontier Vengeance:
Lewis Wetzel and Tom Quick 105

12. Pioneer of Kentucky:
Simon Kenton 113

13. Apekonit, the Linguistic Man of Valor:
William Wells 125

14. Early Mountain Man:
John Colter 133

15. Fur Trader Extraordinaire:
Manuel Lisa 139

Index 155

Illustrations

1. "A new map of North America," 1722 xvi–xvii
2. Radisson and Groseilliers' expedition of 1658–1660 9
3. Radisson and Groseilliers by Frederick Remington 11
4. Radisson and Groseilliers at Hudson's Bay 19
5. Guillaume Delisle map of North America 29
6. Possible locations of Fort d'Orléans 33
7. Location of Saint Louis de Cadodaquious 41
8. Locations of French Rock and Little Rock 45
9. Forts of the La Verendrye expeditions 55
10. La Vérendrye brothers in sight of the western mountains 57
11. Location of the Verendrye lead plate 59
12. The Verendrye lead plate 60
13. Locations of Fort Chartres, Kaskaskia, and Ste. Genevieve 75
14. Attack on Vincennes 89
15. Mackenzie's route to the Arctic Ocean, 1789 95
16. Mackenzie's route to the Pacific Ocean, 1793 101
17. Portrait of Alexander Mackenzie 103
18. Monument to Tom Quick 112
19. A 1784 map of Kentucky 117
20. Engraving of Simon Kenton 121
21. Portrait of William Wells 129
22. Map of North America, 1804 145
23. Portrait of Manuel Lisa 151

INTRODUCTION

How European settlers learned of the vast North American continent was often through the accounts of men who trekked into the wilderness. The chief motivation of these frontiersmen was ascertaining or obtaining natural resources for commerce that took them from the Eastern forests, across the Great Plains, into the Rocky Mountains, or to the Pacific Ocean—years before the celebrated Lewis and Clark Expedition. Their information about Indigenous Peoples, the landscape, and the waterways influenced the course of North American history. While Davy Crockett, Daniel Boone, Kit Carson, and even the fictitious Natty Bumppo of James Fenimore Cooper's *Leatherstocking Tales* are among the most well-known frontiersmen, there were a host of others who deserve as much consideration. They are known chiefly to scholars of early American history, but largely forgotten by the public, even by those interested in early America. This work seeks to bring a few of these ignored yet important figures to greater attention. A number of these figures are Canadian, which may in some degree explain their neglect in the United States. Others were of French origin or derivation, again perhaps explaining why they, too, are often overlooked. One was torn between the French and British, and the other between Indigenous and white societies. One was Spanish. One was a colonial administrator, a force for order in an unsettled world. Two were certainly homicidal. These men are also notable for the fact that, despite their far-reaching voyages, they seldom achieved wealth.

For many years, the chief motivation for these men was beaver pelts, useful because of the unique characteristic of the undercoat hairs of this animal to interlock, forming a felt that was ideal for making hats and waterproof rain garments. Beavers had almost been hunted to extinction in Europe and the Middle East, so the New World beavers were in high demand throughout Europe. Pelts from the northern beavers, particularly those harvested in winter when their coats were at their thickest, were the most desirable. In addition, there has always been curiosity about what exists in unknown regions. What other resources and trade opportunities might there be? These frontiersmen, or explorers as they are commonly labeled, may be described as those who entered an area new to their cultural experience. Indigenous peoples, of course, had long lived in these areas, and were either good trading partners or dangerous foes. Indians had an intimate knowledge of the territory they inhabited and managed, but frequently their knowledge of more distant areas proved unreliable.

The forests of northeastern North America, which appeared to go on forever, gave way to the Great Plains of the Midwest, much to the surprise of the early explorers. While beavers existed even in the prairies, their population did not compare to those of the North. It was not until a market for deerskin leather arose in Europe, used often in bookbinding, that the full resources of the prairies were exploited. Additional resources were soon found across the Midwest, including lead, salt, and buffalo meat, shipped to and eagerly bought in New Orleans and other Eastern locations.

Explorers seldom entered new territories alone. They generally traveled in small groups, sharing the tasks required in making camps, paddling canoes, and occasionally defending themselves. Most contact with Indigenous peoples was peaceful, although occasionally a group would object, sometimes violently, to explorers who would trade guns with other indigenous groups they considered long-standing enemies.

Women seldom took part in explorations. They would remain at home in some settlement, anxiously awaiting the return of their men. The role of these women is too often underappreciated. They had to remain, tending to the children and crops, while the men were absent.

As with our previous volumes on failed European attempts to colonize North and South America, each narrative is supported by discursive commentary on the primary source materials available, indicating where further research might be pursued.[1]

1. *We Could Perceive No Sign of Them: Failed Colonies in North America, 1526–1689* (Westholme Publishing, 2020) and *Neither Hee Nor Any of His Companie Did Return Againe: Failed Colonies in the Caribbean and Latin American, 1492–1865* (Westholme Publishing, 2023).

OVERLEAF: "A new map of North America shewing its principal divisions, chief cities, townes, rivers, mountains &c.," published in 1722. Features include, "Parts as yet unknown," "New Albion, discovered by Sir Francis Drake Anno 1577," "St. Fe or New Mexico, Discovered about 1540, of barren soil and little known," "Part of the Northern Unknown Continent," on this fascinating map. (*Library of Congress*)

A New Map of NORTH AMERICA
Shewing its Principal Divisions, Chief Cities, Townes, Rivers, Mountains &c.
Dedicated
To His Highness WILLIAM
Duke of Glocester.
Scale of English Miles According to Vulgar Computation.
According to Norwood's Computation.
PART OF THE NORT
Arctick Circle
NEW NORTH WALES.
Buttons Bay
NEW SOUTH W
PARTS AS YET UNKNOWN.
Upper L.
Illinois L.
NEW MEXICO or NEW GRANADA,
Discovered about 1540, of a barren soil and little known.
St. Fe or New Mexico.
NEW ALBION discovered by Sir Francis Drake Anno 1577.
CALIFORNIA
GOLF OF CALIFORNIA or VERMILION SEA
HENNEPIN'S DISCOVERY
FLORIDA
Possest by the Spaniards about 1527.
Hotico R.
Holy Ghost R.
Bay of the Holy Ghost.
Coca.
New French Settlement.
GOLF OF MEXICO.
Tropick of Cancer.
St. Iuan.
Culiacan.
St. Michael.
St. Martin.
Zacatecas.
St. Barbara.
NEW BISCAYA.
St. Iago d. Vallos.
Panuco.
St. Iohn d Vlloa.
C. St. Lucas.
Compostella
Aquacara
Guadalajara
Xalisco.
Colima
Mechoacan.
Mexico.
Tlascala
Los Angelos.
Antequera
Chiapa.
MEXICO or NEW SPAIN
Conquered by the Spaniards about 1518. It is stored with Mines of Gold and Silver.
C. Corientes
Acapulco
Sacrificio I.
Bay of Campeachy
P. Royal
Valladolid.
IUCATAN
Vera Pax.
St. Iago d. Guatimala.
St. Salvador.
Leon.
Granada
PACIFICK OCEAN largely taken or the GREAT INDIAN OCEAN, Commonly called by our Sea men the SOUTH SEA.
Abbreviations.
B. Bay. Archb. See.
C. Cape. Bishops See
I. Isle.
M. Mountain.
P. Point.
R. River.

UNKNOWN CONTINENT
GROEN LAND.
ICELAND I.
Davis's Straits
Hudsons Straits
Forbishers Straits
NEW BRITTAIN.
Hudsons Bay
James Bay
Timagaming L.
CANADA
NEW FRANCE.
Canada R.
C. Charles.
Tadousac
St. Johns L.
Quebec
NEW SCOT LAND.
NEW FOUND LAND.
P. Royal
Touquehet.
Sable I.
C. Sable.
NEW ENGLAND
NEW YORK
Ontario L.
Charles T.
Plymouth
Boston.
Milford.
N. London.
Long I.
PENSIL VANIA
Baltimor T.
N. York
VIRGINIA
MARYLAND
NEW JARSEY
James Town
Dellaware R.
Chesepeak Bay.
ENGLISH PLANTATIONS
CAROLINA.
Charles Town.
Edelano
Vitacucha
St. Mathew.
St. Austin.
THE NORTHERN OCEAN, OR SEA.
Bermudas or Summers I.
LUCAIE or BAHAMA ISLANDS
N. Providence
Bahama I.
ANTILLE ISLANDS
Havana
CUBA I. discovered by the Spaniards Anno 1494.
St. Iago.
P. de Martesis.
Tortuga
HISPANIOLA I. Discovered by Columbus A. 1492
St. Dominigo.
C. de Engano.
St. Germans.
PORTO RICO I.
Porto Rico
Angada
Anguilla I.
St. Martin I.
Barbada I.
Antego I.
St. Christophers I.
Guadalop. I.
Dominico I.
THE LEEWARD ISLES.
THE CARIBBEE ISLANDS.
Martinico I.
Barbados
St. Lucia I.
Tabago I.
Trinidada I.
IAMAICA I. discovered by Columbus, taken by the English 1655.
St. Iago.
Port Royal
Vacca or Ash I.
C. de Cruz
C. Gratia dios.
Pearl I.
Andreas I.
Providence I.
Scuda I.
Porto Bello
Conception
Carthago
Panama
St. Fee.
Bay of Panama
CALEDONIA
Cartagena
Rio de la Hacha
St. Martha.
C. de Coquibaco.
Aruba I.
C. Roman
St. Barbara I.
Curasao
Bonairy I.
Aves I.
Blanco I.
Margarita I.
Tortuga I.
N. Corduba.
Orinoque R.
PART of SOUTH AMERICA.

CHAPTER ONE

PRISONER OF THE IROQUOIS, COMPANION OF KINGS

Pierre-Esprit Radisson

(1636/1640–1710)

PIERRE-ESPRIT RADISSON was a complex, chaotic, and somewhat cryptic personality. His own writings are the primary source of most information about his career, supplemented to some degree by records from the Hudson Bay Company. Most of what Radisson wrote is reliable, but often too vague to trace his exact course of travel. His writings also contain some obvious exaggerations, and it has been argued that one early episode is simply not true. Yet what remains is an account of one of the most extraordinary adventurers in the history of North America.[1]

The seventeenth century was an age of faith. Religious wars beset Europe and elsewhere, including North America. Aggressive Jesuits sought to spread what they felt was the only true faith. Amid all of this, Radisson was singularly unconcerned with religion. He was not antireligious; it just simply played only a very small role in his life. Perhaps it was his early exposure to Iroquois beliefs, or perhaps it was just part of his personality, but in his writings, he seldom mentions anything to do with religion. He paid honor to Christianity when occasion and self-interest required, but it seems to have had little to do with his internal life.

By any standard, Radisson lived an event-filled life full of escapades and difficulties, but even his age and birth are matters of doubt. He traced his family to the French town Saint-Malo, but records suggest he was born in the lower Rhône valley near Avignon. In 1697, he reported his age as sixty-one, which agrees with a petition of 1698 in which he gave his age as sixty-two, which would place his birth in 1636. The New France census of 1681, however, gave his age as forty-one, placing his birth in 1640.

1. Radisson's own writings, the basic source for much of his life, can be found in Pierre-Esprit Raddison, *Voyages of Pierre Esprit Radisson: Being an Account of his Travels and Experiences Among the North American Indians, from 1652 to 1684* (Prince Society, 1885). Reissue: Arthur T. Adams, ed., *The Explorations of Pierre Esprit Radisson: From the Original Manuscript in the Bodleian Library and the British Museum* (Ross & Haines, 1961). Also, *Pierre-Esprit Radisson: The Collected Writings*, Germaine Warkentin, ed., 2 vols. (Champlain Society, 2012–2014).

Notable treatments of Radisson's life include Louis Arthur Prud' homme, *Notes Historques sur la vie de P.E. de Radisson* (Imprimerie de L' Agricullure, 1892); Stanley Vestal, *King of the Fur Traders; The Deeds and Deviltry of Pierre Esprit Radisson* (Houghton Mifflin Co., 1940) (a popular work without notes); Grace Lee Nute, *Caesars of the Wilderness: Medard Chouart, sieur des Groseilliers, and Pierre Esprit Radisson, 1618–1710* (Appleton-Century Co., 1943); Berthe Fouchier-Axelsen, ed., *Les aventures extraordinaires d' un coureur des bois. Récits de voyages au pays des Indiens d' Amérique by Pierre-Esprit Radisson* (Éditions Nota Bene, 1999); Martin Fournier, *Pierre-Espirit Radisson: Aventurier et Commerçant* (Septenrion, 2001), English edition, *Pierre-Espirit Radisson: Merchant, Adventurer.* (Septenrion, 2002); and Mark Bourrie, *Bush Runner: The Adventures of Pierre-Esprit Radisson* (Biblioasis, 2019).

Radisson provided one apparently accurate date, his family's migration from France to Canada: May 24, 1651. He arrived with his parents, and his sisters Élisabeth and Françoise and maternal half-sister Marguerite Hayet, who either accompanied their parents or arrived shortly afterward. The family resided in the town of Trois-Rivières where the Saint-Maurice and St. Lawrence Rivers join, southwest of Québec and northeast of Montréal. Marguerite married Jean-Vernon de Grand-Menil in 1646, and the couple had three children. During the seventeenth century, Trois-Rivières was a center of the fur trade and the area around the town still subject to Indian attacks.

During the summer of 1652, Mohawks killed de Grand-Menil near Trois-Rivières. Rapid remarriage was common in French Canada, and so just over a year later Marguerite married Médard Chouart, who had been born about 1621 and migrated to Canada when he was about twenty years old. This was his second marriage also. Médard Chouart assumed the somewhat aristocratic title "Sieur de Groseilliers," perhaps with a hint of irony. "Groseilliers" means literally "gooseberry bushes," the name perhaps derived from a tract of land that he had acquired near Québec on which gooseberry bushes grew in abundance or perhaps from memory of family land in Picardy, where gooseberries also grew. Many French aristocratic or pseudo-aristocratic titles, however, bore geographic references; the first commandment of Fort de Chartres in Illinois bore the name "Boisbriant," Burnt Woods, so perhaps no irony was intended. Henceforth, Médard Chouart was generally known as "Groseilliers." After short intervals as a soldier and a pilot on the St. Lawrence River, Groseilliers entered the fur trade.

In the spring of 1652, while hunting, Radisson had become separated from his two companions, who were killed by Mohawks, the most easterly tribe of the Iroquois Confederacy. Radisson, only in his mid-teens, was captured and spared because of his youth. His willingness to work and to learn the Iroquoian language were viewed positively, and he was adopted into a prestigious Mohawk family as a replacement of a son who had been killed in war.

After an interval of some months, Radisson encountered an Algonquin slave, who convinced him to escape with him. On a hunt,

Radisson, along with three Mohawk companions, camped for the night. During the night, Radisson killed his Mohawk companions—later he would blame the deaths on the Algonquin. Before he and the Algonquin could reach Trois-Rivières, the pair fell into the hands of a Mohawk war party who killed the Algonquin, but again they spared Radisson, probably because he had been adopted into the tribe and the importance of his adoptive family.

Still, Radisson faced ritual torture. His adoptive family warned Radisson to be brave but not too brave. Cowards were slaughtered, and the very bravest were killed so that warriors might eat their hearts and be imbued with their courage. Radisson recorded that the Mohawks made him sing while they pulled out his fingernails and cut, crushed, and burned his fingers, then tied him to a scaffold where he was burned elsewhere, generally abused, and one torturer drove a blade through his foot. He endured three days of this treatment, relatively mild by Mohawk standards, after which his adoptive family compensated other families for the companions who had been killed. After recuperation—it took a month before the puncture through his foot closed—Radisson went on a war expedition that lasted for five months, during which he was carefully watched.

In 1653, Radisson, along with a group of Mohawk warriors, traveled to Fort Orange, today's Albany, New York, for trade. The Dutch then still occupied New Amsterdam, later to be called New York. The Dutch recognized him as French and offered ransom, which Radisson and the Mohawks rejected. Radisson was regarded as a member of the tribe, a Mohawk by adoption, but a Mohawk nonetheless. Radisson, however, was attracted by the notion of returning to European civilization, and in the autumn, he escaped from the Mohawk camp and made his way to Fort Orange. Radisson wrote that he genuinely loved and respected his Mohawk family, but he showed no hesitation in abandoning them.

Radisson made the acquaintance of the Jesuit priest Joseph-Antoine Poncet de La Rivière, and sponsored by the Jesuits, he moved first to New Amsterdam, and then he traveled to Holland, arriving early in 1654. The Jesuits perhaps anticipated that Radisson, now fluent in the Iroquoian language, would join in missionary work.

Once in Holland, however, he quickly proceeded to La Rochelle on the western coast of France. The city was the principal port for New France, and there Radisson was able to find passage on a fishing boat going to the coast of Canada. He traveled with Native Americans from the coast to Quëbec and from there to Trois-Rivières, where his appearance surprised his family who had long regarded him as dead. Radisson had almost certainly met Groseilliers years before, but now he became friends with the older man whom Radisson referred to as his "brother." Groseilliers, however, was a difficult character.

Mark Bourrie, author of a biography on Radisson, refers to Groseilliers as possibly not an altogether trustworthy person:

> The nun Marie de l' Incarnation, who knew Groseilliers well, described him in 1665 as having "a spirit of contradiction and bad humour." She blamed him for the English capture of the Dutch colony in present-day New York State and northern New Jersey, writing that he gave such glowing reports of the place to his friends in Boston that the English became determined to take it, and that he then gave the English advice on how to do so. . . . He had no known loyalties. He also had no social skills or political instincts.[2]

Despite Groseilliers being viewed by some as lacking political instincts and loyalty, Radisson long maintained, and apparently valued, his relationship with him.

The years 1654 to 1656 are often called Radisson's "lost years," and there is much controversy about what he was doing during this period. In 1654, Groseilliers made his first expedition to the West, from which he returned in 1656. He was accompanied by a young man, who many have presumed was Radisson. Radisson claimed to have been on this journey, but some modern historians find his account to be unusually vague. He seems to have written about his adventures while in England during 1668 and 1669, long after the events when memories may have faded. Moreover, Groseilliers oversaw the expedition, and young Radisson's role must have been largely

2. Mark Bourrie, *Bush Runner: The Adventures of Pierre-Esprit Radisson* (Biblioasis, 2019), 79.

restricted to paddling and tasks around the camp such as gathering wood for the fire. Some modern commentators argue that Radisson took no part in the voyage and just wrote himself into the narrative later. A curious document from Québec dated November 1655 bears Radisson's signature, but there is no known reason why he, between fifteen and nineteen years old, would be in Québec at that time and signing a deed. It is likely that the deed has been misdated. Still, no consensus exists about what Radisson was doing from 1654 to 1656.

A short time before Radisson returned to his family the following had taken place: The French had been pressured into "not" keeping peace, with any of the smaller tribes nearby from other Confederacies, by the 'Leading Tribes' within the Iroquois Confederacy who had verbally aligned themselves with the French. The French were to abandon their long-time friends and allies, the Huron and Algonquin, who were still subject to Iroquois attack, as they were then without any help from the French. The Huron had been reduced to little more than a refugee community, and even then, the Onondaga, the leading Iroquois tribe living in what is now central New York State, preyed upon them. Many Huron had settled on the le d' Orléan, within view of Québec. Even so close to this center of French power, the Onondaga still felt free to attack, killing about seventy Huron and abducting enough prisoners to fill forty canoes. The French administration and the Jesuits did nothing substantial to aid the victims. Even the French Jesuits seemed to only help the smaller tribes in order to convert them.

By 1657, the Jesuits established a mission among the Onondaga, at Ste. Marie de Gannentaha. The French organized an expedition to the mission, which included two Jesuit fathers and Radisson, no more than twenty-one years old and perhaps still in his teens. Most of the twenty French on the expedition were soldiers. The voyage also included about eighty Onondaga, around a dozen Huron men, and a hundred Huron women. The Iroquois promised that the Huron could settle peacefully in Iroquois territory. Tensions were high from the beginning of the expedition. Seven of the Iroquois had drowned in an accident at the Lachine Rapids, and the Onondaga were in a foul mood.

In the course of the voyage, the canoe containing Radisson, a Huron man, and two Iroquois men became separated from the main group of the French. Suddenly, the two Iroquois attacked the Huron man, stabbing and shooting him fatally, but they reassured Radisson that he was not in danger. The attack was not an isolated incident. All the Huron men on the voyage were massacred, and the Huron women faced a sad fate as Iroquois slaves. The Onondaga continued to reassure the French that they were in no danger, but one of the Iroquois in Radisson's canoe was a large sullen brute who continually picked fist fights with the much smaller Radisson, much to the amusement of the other Onondaga. The journey was not entirely negative from Radisson's point of view, as he delighted in the abundance of wildlife and the majestic scenery, and strangely did not greatly resent his fights with the large Onondaga man.

When the Onondaga slaughtered the Huron men, they spared one elderly Huron man, Jalack, who had been a famous warrior when younger. Jalack now went among the Onondaga preaching against the French, whom he had come to hate. He told how the French had converted some of the Huron to Christianity while others retained their traditional culture. This deeply divided the tribe, leading to fatal weakness. Jalack claimed that the French had also introduced new diseases among the Huron, killing more than half the tribe. Jalack claimed this would also happen to the Onondaga, and would originate from the mission that the French had established. Jalack's words were received with concern among the Iroquois, and the Jesuits and other French, aware of the Huron's words, feared they could be massacred.

Sometime in early 1658, the French decided to evacuate the mission. They surreptitiously built boats, which they cleverly kept hidden. In preparation for their departure, the French invited the Onondaga to an enormous feast where they fed their guests to excess, and then afterward the French silently fled. The Onondaga did not immediately realize the French had left, assuming they were, like Onondaga themselves, sleeping off the effects of the feast. Radisson recorded that the retreat was difficult. The French left at first thaw. They left at a time when water, used for traveling, was just beginning to thaw, possibly late winter or early spring. However, the weather still remained cold, and the French frequently had to break ice in front of their boats, which would have made traveling quite difficult. It took six weeks to reach Montréal. When the Onondaga awoke and discovered the French were gone, they were so amazed that they concluded they had used magic to disappear.

Groseilliers was preparing another trip to the West, and this time Radisson would accompany him as a partner. Radisson's previous journeys had been of purely personal importance, although they prepared him for his subsequent endeavors. This new venture would change the fate of New France and alter Radisson's life in ways he could not have predicted. The expedition had difficulties from the beginning. The Jesuits wanted Groseilliers and Radisson to take several priests with them, but the partners refused. Priests would only slow their movement and contribute nothing toward their success. Moreover, the Jesuits had ambitions to control as much of the fur trade as possible to raise revenue for their missions. The governor of Montréal also proposed that several of his men, who had no experience in the wilderness, accompany the expedition and receive a large share the profits. Again, the partners refused, but corrupt governmental officials would subsequently prove to be major impediments to the partners' success. They left on the journey under the cover of night.

Leaving from Montréal, the group consisted of Groseilliers and Radisson and a third Frenchman that Radisson never named in his account of events. The partners loaded their boat with axe heads, steel knives, awls, spearheads, iron arrowheads, fishhooks, needles, tobacco, multicolored glass beads, and cloth, all very much in demand by Native peoples. They used all their personal funds, and as much as they could borrow, to purchase trade goods. During the seventeenth century, Native Americans were the chief trappers of beavers, and the prepared hides were traded from tribe to tribe until the pelts came to European trading posts. Each time the furs were traded, they grew more expensive in terms of trade goods. Groseilliers and Radisson hoped to reach the ultimate source of these furs, hunters from the Cree and Sioux (Dakota), and cut out the intermediates who absorbed much of the value.

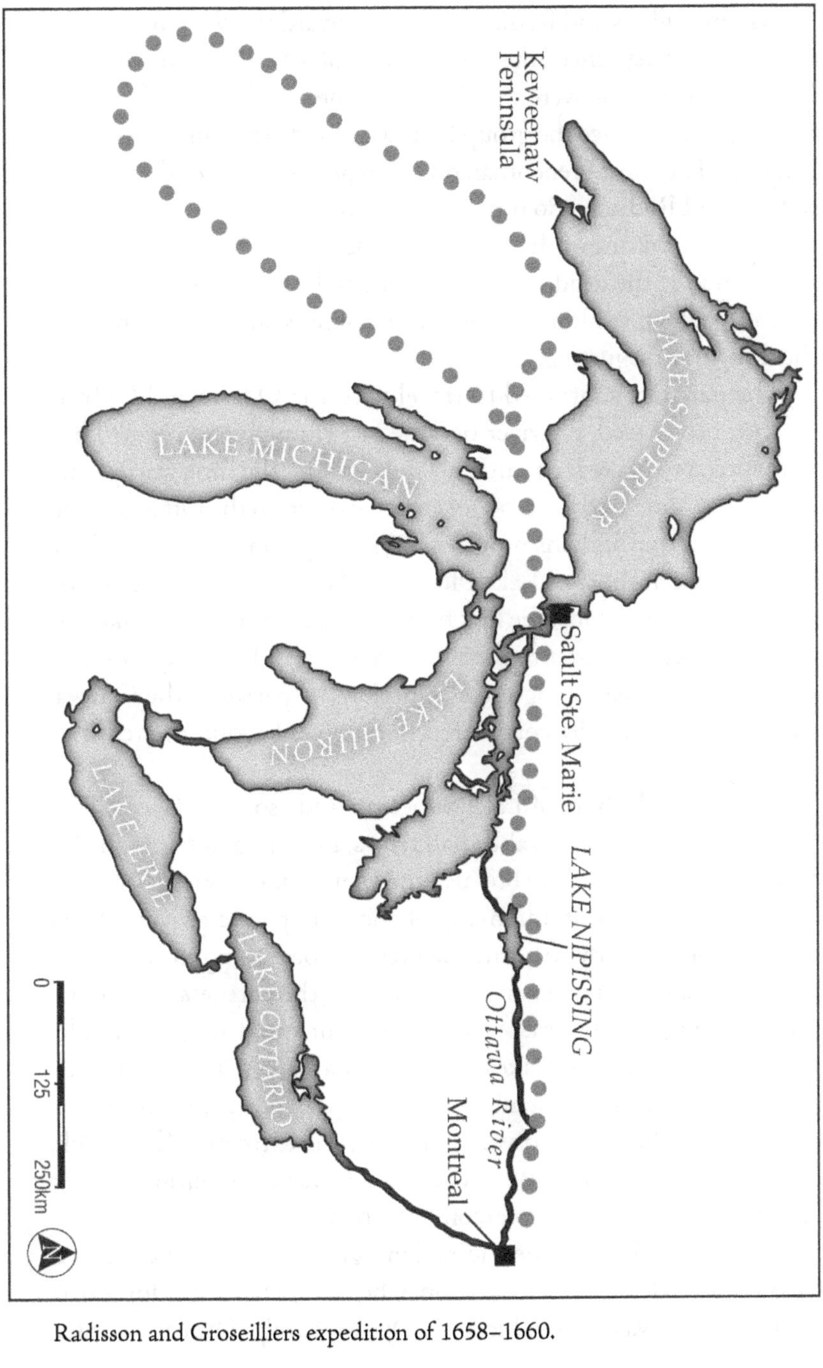

Radisson and Groseilliers expedition of 1658–1660.

As Groseilliers and Radisson set out toward the West on the Ottawa River, they encountered a group of Odawa (Ottawa) and Ojibwe Indians who were traveling the same way. This was fortunate for the partners since the group had two bloody encounters with the Iroquois. The third Frenchman on the expedition deserted, but Groseilliers and Radisson do not seem to have regarded that as a significant loss. After one of the battles, the Odawa and Radisson cooked and ate one of the dead Iroquois. Radisson had been exposed to ritual cannibalism while a captive of the Iroquois and found it neither shocking nor disgusting.

The partners continued to travel with the Odawa and Ojibwe. As they progressed, the river became fast running and rocky. They were forced to make long, difficult portages, all the time warily fearing an encounter with an Iroquois war party. From the Ottawa River, the partners and Indians moved to Lake Nipissing, and from there to the northern shore of Lake Huron, still moving westward. At the Sault Ste. Marie rapids, the link between Lake Huron and Lake Superior, they crossed over to the southern shore of Lake Superior and continued west. Reaching Lake Superior, the partners, the Odawa, and the Ojibwe finally considered themselves beyond the reach of the Iroquois.

On the north shore of Lake Superior, Radisson and Groseilliers were surrounded by several Indian tribes, including not only the familiar Odawa and Ojibwe but also the Menominee, Winnebago, Algonquin, and Potawatomi, many of them desperate refugees from the Iroquois wars. By this time, winter was beginning to set in. On the Keweenaw Peninsula on Lake Superior the partners built a fortified dwelling for the season, a log cabin surrounded by a palisade. They made the entrance lakeside and built a triangular bastion landside. The partners disassembled their canoes and spread the birchbark around the enclosed yard. Birchbark is extremely flammable and will burn vigorously even when wet. It was a precaution against any attackers who might overcome the palisade.

Radisson and Groseilliers joined in a great feast with the Odawa, Ojibwe, and Menominee. Radisson, who always had a gift for learning languages, was adopted into an Ojibwe family. The early winter

Radisson and Groseilliers by Frederick Remington, 1905. Radisson is shown standing with Groseillers sitting beside him. (*Whitney Gallery of Western Art*)

months were a time of plenty and good hunting, but later, heavy snows and low temperatures severely limited hunting, which resulted in hunger. The Indigenous people faced starvation as snow piled up five to six feet deep, and even Radisson and Groseilliers suffered from scurvy. Late in the winter a thaw and refreeze created an ice crust that supported hunters but not deer that were easily killed, relieving the hunger. Later, warm spring rains melted the snow, and those who survived the winter began to revive.

A major event that took place in spring was a great gathering of the many different groups to celebrate the Feast of the Dead. This custom had originated among the Huron but spread to other tribes. Allies would bring the bones of their tribe members who had perished since the previous feast to be mixed and buried together in a great pit, called a "kettle," along with furs and other valuable offerings as symbols of the bond among the tribes. There would also be great feasts, gift giving, and celebrations of the alliances.

Among the Native peoples attending were the Sioux, who at this time lived in permanent settlements. They did not yet have horses, which would change their culture to nomadic buffalo hunters. Radisson did not know the language of the Sioux, and some of the younger warriors were incensed that he and Groseilliers had entered what they considered their country without invitation. The Sioux had obtained guns via trade from the Odawa, and the elders well appreciated the advantage these arms provided in conflict with other tribes. They saw these partnerships as opportunities to acquire more weapons in the future. Radisson and Groseilliers had not included any guns among their trade goods, but the Sioux and others made it clear that they were much desired. Radisson spoke to the Sioux through an interpreter and positioned himself as if he, Radisson, represented all the French and even the royal government in France, promising abundant trade in the near future. Groseilliers and Radisson visited a Sioux village and hunted buffalo with the Indians on foot, a dangerous technique.

During the summer Groseilliers and Radisson traded for beaver pelts and robes with the Sioux, Cree, Ojibwe, and others around the Keweenaw Peninsula. They also traveled south through what is now Michigan, Wisconsin, and even into northern Illinois trading and gathering beaver pelts. During the summer and autumn, Groseilliers also carefully saved a large quantity of dried corn and wild rice; there would be no starvation during their second winter. Radisson, by far the more social of the two, also made plans for a vast fleet of canoes to leave in the spring carrying the many furs they had acquired. They had so many pelts that it would require over one hundred men and a fleet of canoes to transport them. The winter was long and cold, but there was no starvation, and the two men looked forward to returning to Montreal with their enormous store of furs that would surely make their fortunes.

The Cree, fearing the Iroquois, refused to take part in the fleet of canoes, but Radisson managed to convince the Ojibwe and perhaps some Odawa to join. On the way, they encountered the grisly remains of Adam Dollard and his followers hanging from trees; Dollard had come in contact with an Iroquois raiding party. The fact that it was described as grisly, meant that what they found was likely more than a mere hanging.

Groseilliers and Radisson and their canoes carrying the pelts successfully reached the southern edges of what is now known as the

Canadian province of Quebec, choosing to stop in the town of Quebec, south of Montreal, and in a very real sense they saved French Canada. The frontier of French Canada had long needed an ongoing source of income, as they at that time were experiencing a failing economy. French Canada furs had been too few and too expensive to pay expenses, but that changed radically with the arrival of Radisson and Groseilliers. They brought 140,000 pounds of beaver pelts from what is now known as the northern Midwest portion of the United States, all of which would find eager markets in Europe. They were worth about 70,000 livres in a world where a voyageur could be hired for a couple of hundred livres for a year's work. Radisson and Groseilliers, however, could hardly have anticipated what happened next.

The governor at the time was chevalier, Seigneur of Chastre and Vicomte de Mouzay, Pierre de Voyer d'Argenson. 'Provincial governors' were at the time expected to make a profit from their office, but d'Argenson had made little. Some have challenged Radisson's account of what happened next on the basis that he only wrote about it in the late 1680s and then for an English audience enthused to listen to tales of French corruption. Still, there is no doubt that d'Argenson saw this as an opportunity to make his fortune, and he took for himself a good portion of the funds he collected from Radisson and Groseilliers. The two men were fined 4,000 livres by the Governor for having hunted without an appropriate license and the required permission. These fines, supposedly imposed according to royal regulations, were most likely meant to keep absolute control over the trading of furs, as well as line the pocket of d'Argenson. Radisson would later claim that this was done in order to build a new fort at Trois-Rivières, and then 6,000 livres more for general improvements and governmental expenses. Radisson, who refers to the governor as a *bougre*,[3] maintained much of it went into the governor's own account. Then the governor imposed a "trading tax" of an addi-

3. *Bougre* is usually translated as "wretch," "crook," or "villain," but it also generally refers negatively to a person's sexual proclivities.

tional 14,000 livres, much of which, according to Radisson, was also taken by the governor. Still more was consumed in expenses, including trade goods for the several hundred Indians who conveyed the furs to the town of Quebec.

Groseilliers, indignant, quickly left for France to appeal the fine and taxes. He did get much of the fine returned. He was, however, never good with money and lost much of his share of the remaining funds in a failed business scheme, luxurious living, and the importation of half a dozen followers who were supposed to settle at Trois-Rivières in anticipation of future trading expeditions to the West.

Radisson in his account maintains that the theft of much of their profits, ingratitude, and failure to listen to their plans of trading beaver pelts through Hudson's Bay drove the partners to leave New France and go to the English. An additional cause was the hostility of the Iroquois who effectively blockaded the trade routes to the West, probably to protect their profits as intermediaries in the beaver pelt trade from the West. The partners also came into conflict with the Jesuits who wished to dominate the fur trade from Hudson's Bay through the St. Maurice River and James Bay. The Jesuits effectively ended the partners' first attempt to reach Hudson's Bay by sea. It may have been that when the partners reached Port Royal in Nova Scotia, originally settled by the French but now controlled by the English, that they decided their future lay with England, not France. Dealing with the English, however, involved an entirely new set of problems: a rigid class system, a profound distrust of the French, and a deep prejudice against foreigners, especially those who were at least nominally Catholic.

From Port Royal the partners traveled to Boston where they met the Gillam family, ship owners and captains. They would play a major role in the future of Radisson and Groseilliers. Initially, they convinced the Gillam family to sponsor a voyage to Hudson's Bay in order to trade there for beaver pelts. The trip did not prove successful. The captain would not proceed after encountering pack ice south of Baffin Island. They did trade for pelts on the coast of Newfoundland and Labrador, but not enough to make a profit or even cover all the expenses of the journey.

In 1664, Radisson had some good luck. He made the acquaintance of Sir Robert Carr and Colonel George Cartwright, business agent for the 'treasurer of the English Royal Navy,' and George Carteret. The two royal commissioners, Sir Robert and Colonel Cartwright, arranged the English acquisition of what had been New Amsterdam and soon would become New York. Neither the two Frenchmen nor the royalist agents were well received in puritanical Boston, so they naturally gravitated toward one another. Cartwright was enthusiastic about Radisson's plans for trade through Hudson's Bay, and Radisson also held out the possibility that a practical northwest passage could be discovered from the bay to the Pacific and markets in the Far East. In 1665, Cartwright convinced Groseilliers and Radisson to sail to England. Radisson brought along some furs to demonstrate the quality of those available around Hudson's Bay, but the ship was intercepted by Dutch pirates who took everything, including the ship. The passengers and crew were put ashore on a desolate portion of the Spanish coast, and they somehow reached London in December of that year, shortly 'after' the worst of the Plague had devastated the city. That same month, Radisson and Groseilliers were at the royal court. Radisson, much more socially adept than Groseilliers, had now become the dominant partner. Groseilliers merely followed Radisson's lead.

George Carteret, Cartwright's superior, and the aged George Monck, the first Duke of Albemarle, promoted the interests of the partners, and Carteret introduced Radisson to King Charles II. The king seems to have been fascinated by Radisson's stories of his adventures, and the two had much in common despite their very different origins. They were similar in age, and both had passed through dangers and adventures in their past. The king gave Radisson a painted portrait of himself, a gold chain, and support sufficient to provide food and drink for the partners.

Carteret did not long remain as patron to the pair. He was blamed for the poor performance of the English navy against the Dutch and investigated for having embezzled navy funds. The king prevented Carteret's impeachment, but he declined in power and status, and was too busy attempting to salvage his career and fortune to worry much about the two Frenchmen.

Prince Rupert of the Rhine, however, took up the cause of the partners. Rupert was the third son of Prince Frederick V of the Palatinate and Elizabeth, eldest daughter of King James VI of Scotland and I of England, and so a cousin to the king, whom he had served with distinction during the English Civil Wars. Rupert held the titles of Count Palatine of the Rhine, Duke of Cumberland, and Earl of Holderness. He was active, adventurous, artistic, and intellectual. He was also fascinated by Radisson's plan to trade directly through Hudson's Bay and so eliminate transportation through several tribes that absorbed so much of the profit.

The year 1666 brought more adventure. The Dutch and English were at war again. The Dutch had long dominated European commerce, but Britain was a growing economic power. Conflict was inevitable. Radisson's patrons, Rupert and Monck, were both occupied with the English fleet that was fighting epic battles against the Dutch in the English Channel. That was also the year of The Great Fire that consumed most of London. In the aftermath of the fire, rumors persisted that the French and Dutch had set it, inciting mobs to hunt down foreigners. Radisson and Groseilliers, residents at Westminster, were safe from the fire, but mobs lynched Frenchmen wherever they could find them. The partners were lucky to escape that fate.

Reports of Radisson's plans for trade through Hudson's Bay had come to the attention of the Dutch, the French (who regarded the pair as traitors), and the Jesuits. The Dutch and French regarded with alarm the possibilities of such trade that could virtually dominate the fur market. The Jesuits also spied upon the partners. Paul Rageneau, at one time the superior of Jesuits in Canada and procurator of the Canadian mission in Paris, had long been an enemy of Groseilliers whom he regarded as a traitor and probably a heretic as well. Rageneau also regarded Radisson negatively because of his association with Groseilliers and his cooperation with the English. The Jesuits, too, feared English dominance since they relied heavily upon the fur trade to finance their activities. Spies and secret foreign agents surrounded Radisson and Groseilliers and reported every rumor about their plans.

While 1666 was a year of danger, the following several years were ones of frustration for the partners. Groseilliers almost fell victim to a French spy in the service of the Dutch, Godefroy Touret, who befriended him. Touret sought information from Groseilliers and suggested the pair defect to the Dutch. English authorities realized Touret was a spy and arrested him. He attempted to deflect guilt by accusing Groseilliers of a variety of crimes including counterfeiting and concealing a Catholic priest. Fortunately, the accusations were exposed as fantasy, but it became apparent that Groseilliers lacked the sophistication to deal with the dangers of life in England.

Prince Rupert spent much time and effort convincing investors to back Groseilliers's and Radisson's trading expedition to Hudson's Bay. While Rupert gathered supporters, Radisson put pen to paper to record his adventures. He may have begun writing as early as 1666 but probably did not complete his project until about 1669. It is not certain whether he wrote in French or English. His subsequent account of the so-called Fifth Voyage was written in French; the French version survives in the records of the Hudson's Bay Company. Moreover, an employment record exists of a translator. Had he written in English, however, it would explain occasional grammatical obscurity and linguistic lapses. Radisson's writings were not published at the time and almost perished except for a copy held by Samuel Pepys, who worked for the English navy under Prince Rupert.

In 1667, two ships were outfitted for the Hudson's Bay trade, the *Nonsuch*, captained by Zachariah Gillam from Boston and carrying Groseilliers, and the *Eaglet*, carrying Radisson. Groseilliers's ship departed first, but when the *Eaglet* followed it encountered a tremendous storm northwest of Ireland. The sailors had to cut away the main mast to save the ship, after which the ship slowly returned to Plymouth. The *Nonsuch* had more success. Even though it became apparent that Groseilliers had little knowledge of the Hudson's Bay geography, the ship was able to reach Nelson River deep in the bay where they traded with the Cree. As it was too late to return to England, the crew built a fort and settled in for a long, cold winter. Captain Zachariah Gilliam had brought an abundant supply of dried fruit to fend off scurvy, and hunting provided fresh meat. As spring returned, the men traded again with the Cree for furs harvested during the winter and finally left for England in August 1669. The voyage was profitable, delighting the investors, and King Charles II granted the investors a trading monopoly in Hudson's Bay, but Radisson still had not managed to get to Hudson's Bay.

The trading monopoly was the origin of the Hudson's Bay Company, officially incorporated on May 2, 1670.[4] Still operating, the HBC, as it is popularly known, is the oldest incorporated joint-stock merchandising company in the English-speaking world. Also in 1670, another trading journey went to Hudson's Bay. Groseilliers travelled in the *Prince Rupert*, again captained by a member of the Gilliam family, while Radisson sailed on the *Wivenhoe*. A dubious character named Charles Bailey served as governor of the trading journey. He had been a childhood companion of Charles II, but had grown to be a contradictory character, and an intolerant Quaker with a deep hatred of Catholics. His behavior was often obnoxious, and he had been repeatedly jailed in England and on the Continent. He was, however, well organized and ran the fur trade credibly. His hostility toward the partners, however, was manifest, and Bailey hardly mentioned Radisson in any reports, despite Radisson's extraordinary efforts to promote trade with the Cree.

In one sense, Bailey's disregard of Radisson and Groseilliers mirrored the Hudson's Bay Company's evolving view of the partners.

4. For the history of the Hudson's Bay Company, Beckles Willson, *The Great Company (1667–1871): A History of the Honourable Company of Merchant-adventurers Trading into Hudson's Bay* (Smith, Elder and Co., 1900); Charles B. Reed, *Masters of the Wilderness* (Chicago Historical Society, University of Chicago Press, 1914); Douglas MacKay, *The Honourable Company: A History of the Hudson's Bay Company* (Bobbs-Merrill, 1936); Edwin Ernest Rich, *The History of the Hudson's Bay Company, 1670–1870* (Hudson's Bay Record Society, 1958); George Bryce, *The Remarkable History of the Hudson's Bay Company* (B. Franklin, 1968); Peter C. Newman, *Empire of the Bay: An Illustrated History of the Hudson's Bay Company* (Viking Penguin Books of Canada, 1989); Edward Beauclerk Maurice, *The Last of the Gentleman Adventurers* (Houghton Mifflin Co., 2006); Deidre Simmons, *Keepers of the Record: The History of the Hudson's Bay Company Archives* (McGill-Queen's University Press, 2007).

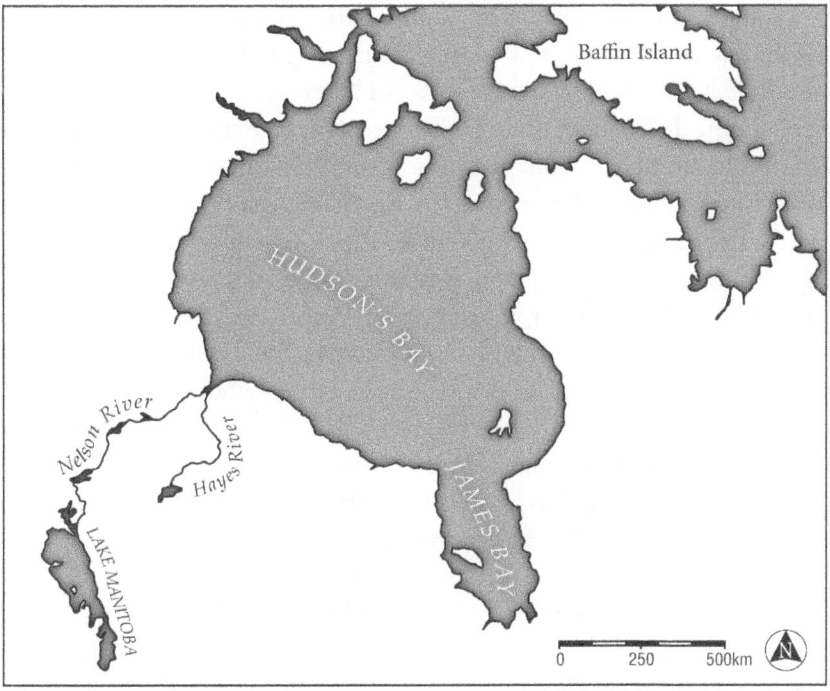

Radisson and Groseilliers at Hudson's Bay. The post was established at the mouth of the Nelson River.

Once the company had gained experience in trading with the Indians and overwintering in the Bay, they had little further use of the pair. English prejudice against the French, and men who were at least nominally Catholic, began to reassert itself. Radisson and Groseilliers could hardly ignore their reduced status in the eyes of the company. They lacked the funds to purchase a share in the company and so had little share in its profits. Back in England, they were each voted the miserable bonus of £5 each, which could hardly be seen as other than a calculated insult. The partners had brought their own trade goods from which they profited a little over £150, but even that was to be prohibited in the future.

The French, alarmed at the English success in Hudson's Bay, sent their own traders there. In 1673, the English sent another trading mission, but discovered the French had already acquired many of the readily available pelts. The English intercepted a Jesuit, Father Charles Albanel. Among his effects was a letter from the French governor Louis de Buade, Comte de Frontenac et de Palluau, generally referred to simply as Frontenac. The letter was an attempt to persuade Groseilliers to defect from the English to the French.

Radisson returned to England, leaving Groseilliers at the Bay engaged in trading. In England, Radisson eloped with and married Mary Kirke, the daughter of a family of Protestant pirates, smugglers, and merchants who had supported the Stuarts and become semi-respectable under Charles II. Mary's father, who disapproved of the marriage, invested in the Hudson's Bay Company and served as one of its directors. Other officials of the company also regarded the marriage critically. Mary found herself in the difficult position of trying to reconcile her father and at the same time remain loyal to her husband, whom she certainly loved.

The anti-Catholic sentiment of the Earl of Shaftesbury, who rose to control the Hudson's Bay Company, and the continuing hostility of Charles Bailey, finally ended the employment of Groseilliers and Radisson. Faced with loss of income in England, they sought reconciliation with the royal French government. In 1675, the French forgave their past disloyalty and welcomed them to France. Radisson hoped to bring his wife to France, but her father virtually imprisoned her to keep her in England. Radisson's inability, or unwillingness, to bring his wife to France cast doubt on Radisson's newly professed loyalty. The partners received a small sum of money from Louis XIV and their debts were paid off, but there was no real employment for them in France. By mid-1676, both were back in Québec, but there was also no apparent role for them there. Groseilliers returned to his wife and son near Trois-Rivières. He had shamefully neglected them for years, but they welcomed him back. The family eked out a living by farming and smuggling furs.

Radisson returned to France where he joined the marines. France and the Netherlands, formerly allies against England, were now at war with one another. In 1676, Jean d'Estrées (II), Comte d'Estrées, led a disastrous naval campaign in an attempt to conquer the isle of

Tobago, then held by the Dutch. He landed a force of 750 men on the island, greatly outnumbering the Dutch defenders. A great naval battle at Rockley Bay ensued, during which fire spread throughout the two fleets. The Dutch fleet was almost completely destroyed as were all but four of the French warships. On land, the outnumbered Dutch badly defeated the French force whereupon d'Estrées gathered the survivors and sailed for home. Radisson was lucky not to have taken part in this disaster, but he participated in d'Estrées's second campaign against Tobago and other Dutch held islands in the Caribbean, and even invested money in the expedition. It could be anticipated that the French fleet would indulge in some privateering and turn a profit, and to that end they enlisted pirates who sailed in their own ships as part of the fleet.

In the second campaign, D'Estrées landed five hundred men at Rockley Bay who attacked the Dutch fort with artillery. A mortar round set off the Dutch fort's powder supply, virtually annihilating the fort and killing most of the officers and many of the garrison. The French had Tobago, but d'Estrées's fleet was soon destroyed by one of the worst naval disasters in French history.

The Las Aves archipelago is a small group of islands about eighty miles off the coast of Venezuela, mostly surrounded by coral and rock reefs. D'Estrées's fleet sailed near these islands on a dark and moonless night on their way to attack the Dutch island of Curaçao. Reports differ about what happened next. Some claim that Dutch ships cleverly lured the French fleet onto the reefs, while others maintain that the pirate ships, sailing in advance of the main fleet, simply blundered into the islands. When the first pirate ships hit the reef, they fired a cannon to warn the main fleet, but the shot had just the opposite effect. Thinking the advanced ships had encountered the enemy, the main fleet made full sail and crashed into the reefs. Ships encountering sand just below the water would have sunk deeply, as if it were quick sand, and this most likely having destroyed the underside of these wooden vessels would have made it impossible for them to sail again. A moonless night meant that the phase of the moon was a new moon when any incoming tides are extremely low; ships would have been incapable of movement. A few of the smaller ships sailing behind the main fleet must have managed to stay back, avoiding this particular danger, as several small ships did manage to leave and return weeks later for survivors. Most of the fleet was destroyed that very night by the coral and rock reefs, which ripped hulls open and sank all the larger ships—virtually the entire effective force of the French fleet. Most of the pirates made it ashore, as did Radisson. Rough men, they quickly salvaged barrels of salt meat and wine. Radisson and the pirates seem to have fared well while awaiting rescue, but many of the French sailors and soldiers who clambered to shore died there. Radisson, however, always traveled with hard cash, having no faith in banks, however, it went down with the ship.

D'Estrées, having left on one of the surviving ships, returned about three weeks later to rescue the survivors, including Radisson. Radisson returned to France, raised a little money from supporters, and traveled to England where he unsuccessfully attempted to convince his father-in-law to allow his wife to join him in France. Back in France, without funds or resources, Radisson appealed to the Marquis de Seignelay, the son of Jean-Baptiste Colbert, First Minister of State. Again, his wife's continuing residence in England cast doubts on Radisson's loyalty, and he received no aid.

In 1681, Radisson returned to Canada and met with his old partner, Groseilliers, who was now somewhere around sixty years old, elderly by the standards of the age. Radisson said he was forty-one that year, but he may not have known the exact year of his own birth. The pair plotted an expedition to Hudson's Bay to trade for beaver pelts. It would have to be fast and surreptitious to avoid Hudson's Bay Company crews and New Englanders hungry for beaver pelts. The partners arranged transport on two small sloops, the *St. Pierre* and *Ste. Anne*, manned by surly crews.

Shortly after arriving, Radisson and his small group encountered a group of New Englanders led by old Zachariah Gillam and his son Benjamin. Zachariah had become a sworn enemy of Radisson and Groseilliers after their defection to the French. Radisson also confronted men from the Hudson's Bay Company led by John Bridgar. Radisson played a duplicitous game by lying. He claimed that he had many more men, a strong fort, and several ships, far more than necessary to dominate either the Gillams or the Hudon's Bay Company. Both were deceived by Radisson's bravado. Meantime, the Cree were impressed by Radisson's ability to speak their language, and even when they realized that he was giving less for pelts than others were doing elsewhere, he was able to talk his way out of the conflict. Zachariah Gillam was killed when ice pushed his grounded ship out to sea and crushed it. Radisson finally gave Bridgar a small boat, a few provisions, and set him and a small crew to sea in order to row to a distant port. They were rescued at sea and subsequently sued Radisson but got no satisfaction. Radisson brought Benjamin Gillam and his men to Québec, where Governor Joseph-Antoine le Fèbvre, sieur de La Barre, freed them.

Shortly after arriving at Québec, the partners received a letter from First Minister of State Jean-Baptiste Colbert, ordering their appearance at Versailles to explain and justify their actions. Clearly, the French government did not want a war with England and feared the two might have deeply provoked the English. Colbert had always favored Radisson and had deflected criticisms of him, but by the time the partners reached France, Colbert had died, and the two were left without an advocate. Neither France nor England, however, were eager for a war over a cold coast and beaver pelts. Charles II of England was also secretly receiving massive bribes from Louis XIV and wanted nothing to alter the situation. No one in France was eager to finance another trade mission to Hudson's Bay, and so there was no future for the partners in France.

The Hudson's Bay Company wanted Radisson and Groseilliers in its employ, not because it had any project for the pair, but rather out of fear of what the pair might be planning in France. Groseilliers declined the offer and returned to his farm near Trois-Rivières. It is not certain how long he survived, perhaps as late as 1696. Radisson accepted and returned to the Bay in 1684. There he tricked Jean-Baptiste Chouart, Groseilliers's son, to surrender the post and the enormous hoard of twenty thousand furs he had accumulated. Radisson did get Chouart and his crew employment with the company, and all returned to the Bay in 1685 for more trading that continued for several more years. Radisson's wife, Mary Kirke, died in

1685, and, typically for the age, Radisson did not remain a widower for long, marrying Charlotte Godet in 1686. That was also the year of Radisson's last trip to Hudson's Bay. Subsequently he retired to London, but the Hudson's Bay Company proved ungrateful. It refused him a job as the London warehouse keeper and even attempted to reduce his pension, although after extensive legal litigations he won the original pension. Radisson died in London in 1710, about seventy years of age or a little older.

CHAPTER TWO

ROGUE, MISSOURI RIVER PIONEER, NOBLEMAN

Étienne de Véniard de Bourgmont

(1679–1734)

Étienne de Véniard de Bourgmont was born in 1679 at Cerisy-Belle-Étoile in the Normandy region of France.[1] His name hints at upper-class origins. His father was a respected surgeon, and his great-uncle was the grand vicar of the bishop of Québec. His father died while Bourgmont was young, and his mother remarried. Evidently, his stepfather was not as respectable as his father. When Bourgmont was nineteen years old he, his step-

1. Etienne Véniard de Bourgmont is well-known to historians but much less so to the public despite his wide-ranging explorations and extraordinary exploits. Basic biography includes Henry Folmer, *Etienne Veniard de Bourgmond in the Missouri County* ([n.s.]: [n.p], 1942); F. Norall, *Bourgmont, Explorer of the Missouri, 1698–1725* (University of Nebraska Pres, 1988); David MacDonald, *Lives of Fort de Chartres: Commandants, Soldiers, and Civilians in French Illinois 1720–1770* (Southern Illinois University Press, 2016), 130–37 and materials cited there.

father, and uncle were caught poaching on the grounds of the monastery at Cerisy. He was fined 100 livres, but rather than pay that substantial sum, young Bourgmont absconded to Canada, where he joined the French Marines. In 1702, Charles Juchereau de St. Deny, not to be confused with the more famous Louis Juchereau de St. Deny, established a tannery for buffalo hides near the confluence of the Wabash River and the Ohio River. St. Deny commanded a contingent of the French Marines that included Bourgmont, who may have held the position of cadet, officer in training. Unfortunately, the tannery was not a success and was closed in 1703 when St. Deny died.

By 1705, Bourgmont held the rank of ensign, the lowest ranking officer, and served under Antoine Laumet de la Mothe Cadillac at Fort Pontchartain de Detroit. Cadillac, always interested in advancing his career, traveled to France in 1706 and left Bourgmont as interim commander of the fort. It was irresponsible of Cadillac to leave such a young and inexperienced man in command, especially as the Ottawa and Miami tribes both camped around Detroit were engaged in a long-standing feud. A series of increasingly violent confrontations between the two tribes took place over several months, culminating when a group of Ottawa attacked the Miami. The Miami and some Huron fled to the fort, which allowed them to enter. The Ottawa then attacked the fort, and Bourgmont had the garrison, joined by the Miami and the Huron, fire on the Ottawa, killing about thirty of them. That might have been forgivable, but a missionary priest and a French sergeant were also killed in the encounter. Cadillac blamed Bourgmont for failure to avoid the conflict, but Bourgmont was a young officer with no experience in intertribal diplomacy, and Cadillac was always skillful in deflecting blame from himself. Cadillac sent a very critical report of Bourgmont's conduct to Philippe de Rigaud, Marquis de Vaudreuil, the governor general of Canada, who harshly criticized Bourgmont for failure to control the Indians and resolve the conflict peacefully.[2]

2. Norall, *Bourgmont*, 8–11; S. Vincens, *Madam Montour et sons temps* (Québec/Amérique, 1979) and in English in S. Vincens, *Madam Montour and the Fur Trade (1667–1752)*, trans. and ed. R. Bernstein (Xlibris, 2011), 157–162.

At this point, Bourgmont entered the most mysterious period of his life. Officially, before the end of 1706, he and a number of enlisted men deserted to lead the lives of coureurs de bois, literally "woods runners," unlicensed (and hence illegal) trappers and Indian traders. A woman who had been widowed in the attack on the fort, Madame Montour, also left with Bourgmont. She would go on to have an independent career as a famous translator and negotiator between the Indians and the French, and later between the English and the Indians.[3]

Yet there were elements that suggest that all was not as it appeared. Bourgmont was never recorded as a deserter, and continued to be listed as an officer of the marines. There seems to have been little attempt to apprehend him, and rumors circulated that he was functioning as an undercover agent, reporting on the Indians around the Great Lakes, in the Illinois Country, and in Missouri. Other rumors claimed he was Cadillac's private agent, trading illegally with the English for Cadillac. Cadillac was certainly capable of such fraudulent behavior. Even Cadillac's aristocratic sounding name was an invented fake. There is, however, no evidence to support the rumors.

Whatever the truth, for six years Bourgmont and his merry men certainly fulfilled the image of the coureurs de bois. They partnered with Indian women, drank, partied, brawled, and scandalized every settlement they visited. Bourgmont entered into a Native marriage with a Missouri woman who bore him a son. The Jesuit clergy wrote strong letters of complaint to France, and the royal court instructed the governor general of Canada to deal with Bourgmont and his band. Bourgmont and his men, however, were away in the Western woods, far from the power of even the governor general of Canada. Bourgmont even made a visit to Mobile. Cadillac was then governor of Louisiana, and the French king ordered Bourgmont's arrest, but by the time the ordered arrived, Bourgmont had returned to Missouri.

Yet redemption was close at hand. Bourgmont wrote two reports about the geography of the Mississippi and Missouri Rivers. The

3. MacDonald, *Lives*, 134; Norall, *Bourgmont*, 99–123.

first was entitled "The Route to Be Taken to Ascend the Missouri River." It contains little text, but includes distances, compass headings, and landmarks from the mouth of the river to the juncture with the Platte River, 635 miles. The work is so exact that the cartographer Guillaume Delisle was able to rely upon it to produce a good map of the river. The second work is more discursive: "Exact Description of Louisiana, of its Harbors, Lands and Rivers, and the Names of the Indian Tribes That occupy it, and the Commerce and Advantages to be Derived Therefrom for the Establishment of a Colony."[4]

Much of the information about southern Louisiana was not new, but the exact account of the Mississippi River, its major tributaries, and the Indian tribes as far north as the Platte River was of great value. Bourgmont also included less detailed material about the Missouri River and tribes even farther upstream as far as South Dakota.

These two works made it apparent that Bourgmont was the fundamental source about Missouri, and Missouri was important to the French Crown and to the Compagnie des Indes, which at that time controlled Louisiana as a royal concession. Missouri had become a valuable source of fine furs and skins that brought considerable income to Louisiana, and the French wanted their Indian traders and trappers to be able to function in Missouri peacefully. The French were also concerned about the intrusion of the Spanish into the area. Both nationalities wanted to trade with the Indian tribes in the area, though the Indians much preferred the quantity and quality of French trade goods. Still, the Spanish penetration into the area was alarming. In 1720, the Spanish Villasur expedition penetrated as far north as Nebraska, but there the Pawnee and Otoe disastrously massacred the Spanish; only a few survivors returned to Santa Fe.

After the publication of Bourgmont's two works, past sins were evidently forgiven, and he was no longer regarded as a wanted fugitive. Indeed, the rapidity with which Bourgmont went from outlaw to honored servant of the Crown hints that his interval as a coureur

4. Norall, *Bourgmont*, 99–123, gives translations of Bourgmont's two works.

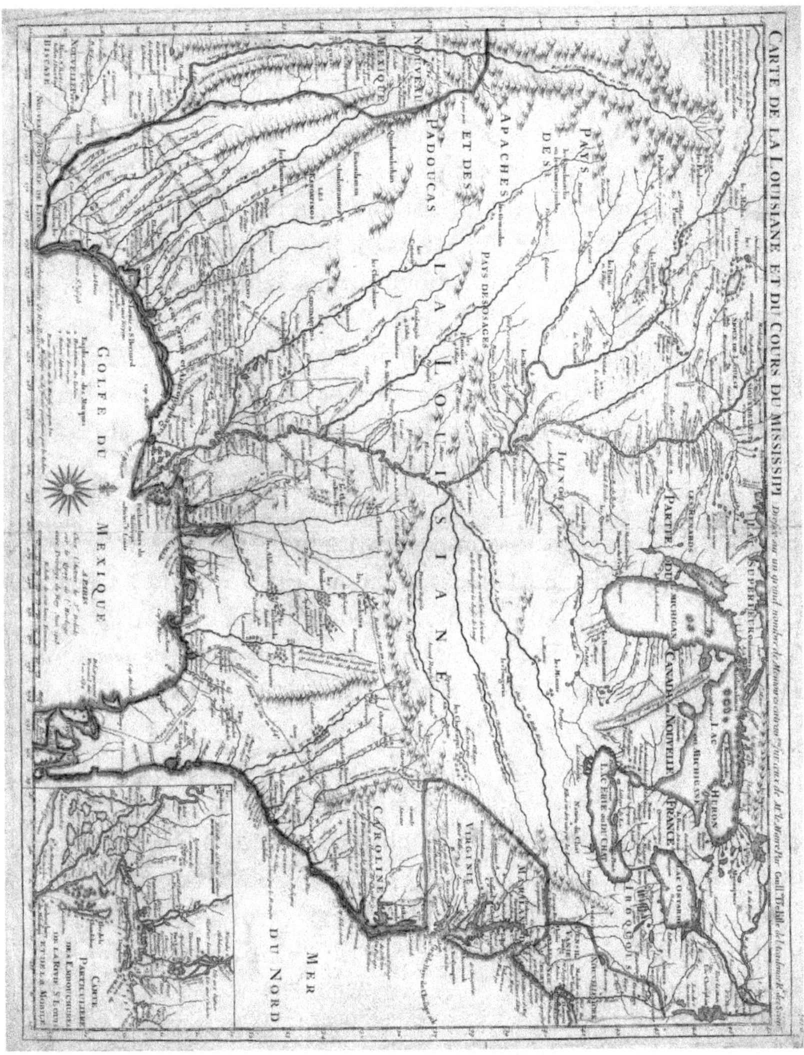

The 1718 map of North America produced by Guillaume Delisle based upon Bourgmont's information. (*Library of Congress*)

de bois was not all that it was reported to be. From 1714 to 1718, Bourgmont seems to have represented French interests in Missouri, and in 1718, he brought a group of chiefs of the Illinois and Missouri tribes to Dauphin Island near Mobile, then the French administrative center, to reinforce the alliances with the French. The delegation proved a disaster as disease broke out among the group, killing all but one Indian. Bourgmont conveyed the survivor back to his tribe and brought abundant gifts to compensate for the deaths.

In 1720, Bourgmont went to France along with his son by the Missouri Indian woman. In that same year, the enthusiasm for investing in Louisiana, later known as the "Mississippi Bubble," was at its height in France and throughout Europe. John Law, the Scottish economist, had convinced the French court to support his Banque Royale, which also controlled the Compagnie des Indes. Promotion had convinced a wide variety of people of all classes that Louisiana and the Mississippi River valley contained incredible wealth, and stock prices rose to unimaginable levels before the "Bubble" burst, after which stock prices collapsed, and Law fled from France. Nevertheless, the Crown and Compagnie des Indes retained an interest in Missouri, and that benefited Bourgmont. He was granted the rank of captain in the Royal Marines, awarded the Grand Cross of the Order of St. Louis, and appointed Commandant of the Missouri River. While in France, Bourgmont also married a French widow, who brought a substantial dowry.[5]

Leaving his new wife in France, Bourgmont returned to Missouri in 1721 with an impressive set of orders. He was to promote peace among the Indian tribes, and establish trade with the Spanish, but at the same time establish a post on the Missouri River to prevent Spanish intrusion into the area. Bourgmont was also to arrange a visit of tribal leaders to France. Once all of this was accomplished, Bourgmont was promised to receive promotion to the aristocracy.

The Missouri Indians thought so highly of Bourgmont that a large group traveled three hundred miles to greet him in Illinois.

5. MacDonald, *Lives*, 137; Norall, *Bourgmont*, 99–161.

Bourgmont's first task was to establish Fort d' Orléans on the Missouri River. The exact location of the fort has never been found, and speculation about it has become a favorite occupation of modern writers. The best evidence indicates that the fort was in the vicinity of the confluence of the Grand River and the Missouri, perhaps on an island five miles to the south or on a bluff two miles south of the town of Miami, Missouri, or perhaps by a nearby prairie. The Missouri and Grand Rivers have flooded many times since the 1720s, reshaping the landscape. A large portion of the island has washed away and reformed, the bluff has eroded, and the prairie subject to long habitation by Indians after the destruction of the fort, in addition to frequent inundations and modern agricultural use. It is quite possible that the exact location of the fort may have been completely eradicated by nature and human activity.[6]

From Fort d' Orléans about or during 1722, Bourgmont set out to meet with the Padouca, but a disease struck the expedition and Bourgmont, among others, fell ill. He soon recovered, however, and in a second attempt reached the plains of central Kansas, where he was able to arrange peace between the Padouca, the Missouri, and other tribes allied to the French. In 1724, Bourgmont arranged for a delegation of Indians to visit France, which consisted of four chiefs of the Missouri, four chiefs of the Osage, one chief of the Oto, and a number of interpreters and other native dignitaries, and the daughter of the paramount Missouri chief. The French rendered the daughter's name as Ignon Ouaconisen. They were supposed to be joined by five chiefs of the Illinois tribes and Pierre-Sidrac Dugué de Boisbriand, the commandant of Illinois, but the governor of

6. Millard Fillmore Stipes, *Fort Orleans on the Missouri: Its Location and History, with Some Accounts of Bourgmont's Expeditions to the Padoucas* (Gazette Office, 1906). This work is obsolete in many particulars and relies too much on English translations rather than consulting the French originals, but the discussion of the location of Fort d' Orléans remains relevant. Also, Marc de Villiers du Terrage, *La decouverte du Missouri et l' historie du Fort d' Orleans: 1673–1728* (Libraire ancienne Honore Champion, 1925). For the identification of the Padouca as Apache rather than Commanche, see George Bird Grinnell, "Who were the Padouca?" *American Anthropologist*, (n.s.) 22, no. 3 (July–September, 1920): 247–60.

Louisiana, Jean-Baptiste Le Moyne Bienville, had been recalled to France, and Boisbriand had to assume the position of interim governor. So the chief Jesuit of Illinois, Father Nicolas-Ignace de Beaubois, took Boisbriand's role. This created difficulties as Beaubois was a haughty, tactless man with a profound dislike of military officers and a lingering dislike of Bourgmont stemming from his years as a coureur de bois. He disassociated himself from Bourgmont, and he and the Illinois chiefs traveled separately. When all got to Dauphin Island, the authorities realized that the costs to transport and support such a large group would be excessive, so the group was limited to just five chiefs, Ignon Ouaconisen, an Indian slave as servant, Sergeant Dubois, Bourgmont, and Father Beaubois, who had to travel with Bourgmont despite his dislike for him. Four of the chiefs were from the Missouri tribes and just one from the Illinois.

The trip to France began badly. The ship on which they initially sailed hit some floating logs and was so badly damaged that it had to return to the Dauphin Island anchorage where it sank. The Indians were distressed that all the gifts that they brought for the king and officials of the Compagnie des Indes were lost. During the subsequent voyage to France on another ship, one of the Missouri chiefs died. The rest of the party arrived in late September 1725.

In France, the Indians were shown Paris and the great palaces at Versailles and Marly, and they were duly impressed. King Louis XV, only fifteen years old, was fascinated by the Indians, and at the Château de Fountainebleau the Indians hunted deer in the royal forest for the entertainment of the king and court. Ignon Ouaconisen was the source of much speculation as women in France were not part of the political world. Her father had sent her as his representative as he did not feel he could leave the Missouri at that time since the tribe was involved in a brutal war with the Fox. The chiefs were given court dress and shown how to wear it. Ignon Ouaconisen was gowned in a dress described as the color of fire and decorated with golden flowers. While in Paris, she officially converted to Catholic Christianity, was baptized in Notre-Dame Cathedral, and given the baptismal name Françoise Missouri. Shortly thereafter she married Sergeant Dubois in the same cathedral. Dubois was given an "ex-

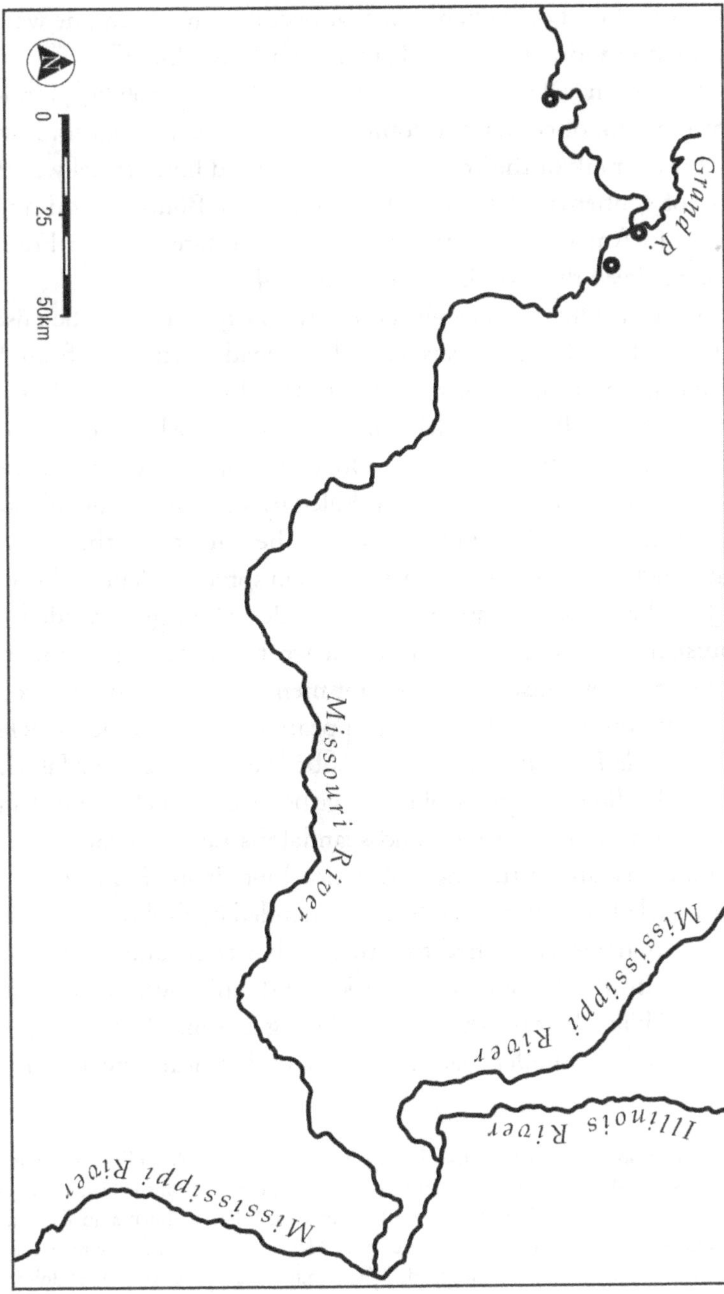

Possible locations of Fort d'Orléans.

pectancy of ensign." When next that post became vacant, he would receive promotion to that rank, making him an officer.[7]

Bourgmont also received a promotion: a letter of nobility granting him the rank of écuyer, the equivalent of "squire" in English. It was the lowest rank of the aristocracy, but it raised him officially to the rank of gentleman, far above the commoners. Bourgmont did not return to America but rather retired to an estate with his French wife. He lived there until his death in 1734.

Sergeant Dubois, now with the certain expectation to be raised to the rank of officer, conveyed the chiefs, loaded with gifts from the royal court and the Compagnie des Indes, along with his wife, similarly laden, to Illinois and Missouri. The marriage between Dubois and Françoise Missouri survived long enough for her to bear two children, but in 1728 Dubois was killed by Indians. No details survive about the incident, but at that time the war against the Fox was at its height, and he may well have fallen in some incident of the war.

Jean-François-Benjamin Dumont de Montigny resided in Louisiana from 1719 to 1738, and he wrote an account of his time there. In the manuscript he did not mention Dubois or Françoise Missouri, but in 1753 his journal appeared in print as *Mémoires historique sur la Louisiane*, edited by l' Abbé Jean-Baptiste Le Mascrier. The Abbé did not approve of marriage between French and Indians, and he interpolated a false and scandalous tale into the memoir claiming that after returning to America, Dubois and Françoise Missouri settled at an unnamed fort commanded by Dubois. Françoise Missouri, however, wished to return to her tribe, and so she conspired with the Indians who attacked suddenly, overwhelmed the fort, and killed Dubois and the rest of the garrison. The story is pure fiction, and a reminder that in the eighteenth century the writing of

7. For contemporary reports of the visit see, "Relation de l' arrivée en France de quarte Sauvages du Missisippi, de leur sjour, & des audiences qu' il ont euës du Roi, des Princes du Sang, de la Compaagnie des Indesm avesc les compliments qu' ils on fair, les honneurs & les prends au' il ont reçûs &c.," *Mercure de France* I (December 1725): 2828, and C. J[ordan], "Les Sauvages de l' Amerique ont audience du Roy et doivert s' en retourner den leur pays," *Suite de la Clef, ou Journal historique sur les matières du temps* 19 (February 1726): 209–10.

history was not so much a quest for the truth as an opportunity to teach moral lessons, to entertain, and to sell books.[8] The truth is that soon after Dubois's death, Françoise Missouri married Louis-Hector Marin de La Malgue, the captain of the militia at New Chartres. The couple had three children, and Françoise Missouri lived in the French community until her death in 1739. Marin raised the children born to Dubois along with his own from a previous relationship. Individuals who can trace their ancestors to Françoise Missouri still live in Missouri.

8. For Dumont's original unaltered text see, J.-F.-B. Dumont de Montigny, *Regards sur le monde atlantique, 1715–1747*, eds. C. Zecher, G. M. Sayre, and S. L. Dawdy (Septentrion, 2008). For the altered text see, J.-F.-B. Dumont de Montigny, *Mémoires historique sur la Louisiane* "Composés sur les Mémoires de M. Dumont par M. L' Abbé Le Mascrier" (C.-J.-B. Bauche, 1753).

CHAPTER THREE

EXPLORER OF THE SOUTH

Jean-Baptiste Bénard, Sieur de la Harpe

(1683–1765)

JEAN-BAPTISTE BÉNARD DE LA HARPE'S involvement in exploration was of short duration, but nonetheless important. He explored the Red River at a time when the river was not yet settled by the French. The river, in part, lay along the New Spain and Louisiana border. In only a few years' time he increased knowledge of geography and peoples, and helped form a better understanding involving trade along the borders between the French and Spanish.

La Harpe was born early in 1683 at Saint-Malo, France, one of twelve children (five sons and seven daughters) of Pierre Benard, Seigneur de la Harpe and Jeanne le Breton. La Harpe was the second born son, but his older brother died at a young age. His father died when la Harpe was only ten years old. His family was upper class but not one of the true elite families of France. He received a good education and later proved himself a skilled author. In 1701, la

Harpe became a junior officer in a Spanish cavalry regiment, but his family called him back home after only a short time for an unknown reason, so he resigned and returned to Saint-Malo.

Shortly after returning home, la Harpe sailed as an ensign, the lowest rank of officer, on one of three ships which set out on an exploration voyage to Peru. The Spanish did not permit their colonies to trade with foreigners, but Spain failed to provide her colonies with sufficient goods. Local, and even royal officials, contrived elaborate evasions of the trade laws. For example, a captain might claim that his ship had been badly damaged in a storm and required repairs. He would also claim that he needed to sell some of his cargo in order to pay for the renovations. A choice portion of the cargo would, of course, be sold to the cooperating official for a pittance. In port, la Harpe gained permission to go inland to visit the rich mines of Peru. He remained inland for five months, and by the time he returned to the coast, his ship had long sailed for home. La Harpe had taken the precaution of warehousing a significant amount of goods from the ship's stores, and so he set himself up as a merchant in Peru. While there, in 1705, he married a wealthy widow, Doña María de Rokafull. She had originally come from Flanders and was twenty-two years older than la Harpe. It was not a happy union. La Harpe had exaggerated his assets to the bride, and she condemned his account of his experiences in South America as a work of fiction. Although there is no known surviving copy of la Harpe's "first" venture in publishing, he would eventually put pen to paper in describing his later explorations along the Arkansas River, and in helping to establish French Louisiana. The couple moved to France in 1706 but matters deteriorated to the point where María attempted to have the marriage annulled. Such attempts take considerable time to move through the complex bureaucracy, and the case had still not been fully adjudicated when María died in 1709. Her heirs successfully prevented la Harpe from inheriting her wealth. La Harpe soon married again, but his second wife died a few years later.[1]

1. See A. L. Boimare, ed., Jean-Baptiste Bénard de la Harpe, *Journal Historique de L' Établissement des Français a La Louisiane* (Hector Bossange, 1831). Some have argued

In 1718, la Harpe sailed to French Louisiana. He obtained a concession from the Compagnie des Indes (Company of the Indies), which managed the Louisiana colony. Sources disagree whether he held a grand concession of four square leagues, about thirty-six square miles, or just six small concessions, but they do agree that the land was on the Red River, an area not yet settled by the French. La Harpe had been accompanied to Louisiana by about forty men eager to settle in the new land.

In obedience to orders from the governor, la Harpe proceeded up the Red River. He paused briefly at Natchitoches, founded two years previously by Claude-Charles du Tisné. Traveling upriver through many difficulties, la Harpe established early in 1719 Fort Saint Louis de los Cadodaquious (spelled various ways) in the vicinity of modern Texarkana, at an oxbow lake formerly part of the Red River, now called Roseborough Lake. The fort was established near a village of

that Jean de Beaurain, the king's geographer, combined a number of la Harpe's memoires to produce the work; it is available in English as Jean-Baptiste Bénard de La Harpe, *Historical Journal of the Settlement of the French in Louisiana* (United States Library of Congress, 1851). La Harpe's account has frequently been criticized as unreliable. For example, his claim that he visited an Indian village with a population of six thousand was criticized as unbelievable, but George H. Odell et al.'s *La Harpe's Post: A Tale of French-Witchita Contact on the Eastern Plains* (University of Alabama Press, 2002) has shown the estimate to be quite reasonable. Also, see Pierre Margry, *Découvertes et Établissement des Français dans l' ouest et le sud de l' Amérique du Nord*, vol. 6 (Maisonneuve et Cie, 1888) for a fuller publication of la Harpre's memoires of his explorations on the Red and Arkansas Rivers. For general bibliography see Marc de Villiers du Terrage, *An Explorer of Louisiana: Jean-Baptiste Bénard de la Harpe (1683–1765)* (Ouachita Baptist University Institute for Regional Studies, 1983). French version: Marc de Villiers du Terrage, *Un Explorateur de la Louisiane. Jean-Baptiste Bénard de la Harpe, 1683–1765* (Bibliothèque nationale du Québec, 1988). This work was originally published in 1934. Specific studies include M. P. Miroir, R. K. Harris, J. C. Blaine, and J. McVay, "Bénard de la Harpe and the Nassonite Post," *Bulletin of the Texas Archaeological Society* 44 (1973): 113–67; Mildred Mott Wedel, "J.-B. Bénard, Sieur de La Harpe: Visitor to the Wichitas in 1719," *Great Plains Journal* 10 (1971): 37–70; Mildred Mott Wedel, "La Harpe's 1719 Post on Red River and Nearby Caddo Settlements," *The Bulletin of the Texas Memorial Museum* 30 (1978); Jean-Baptiste Bénard de La Harpe, "Exploration of the Arkansas River by Benard De La Harpe, 1721–1722: Extracts from His Journal and Instructions," Ralph A. Smith, trans. and ed., *The Arkansas Historical Quarterly* 10, no. 4 (Winter 1951): 339–63; Pierre Heinrich, *La Louisiana sous La Compagnie des Indes* (Burt Franklin, 1908).

the Nasoni Indians, a tribe of the Caddo Nation. Moving beyond the new installation, la Harpe founded a post farther upstream, the so called Nassonite Post. From there he sent communications to the Spanish, hoping to establish a profitable trade, but France and Spain were in conflict as part of the War of the Quadruple Alliance. The French also raided the Spanish San Miguel de Linares de los Adaes mission, one of the relatively nearby Spanish settlements. The Spanish authorities generally prohibited trade with the French, and the state of war destroyed any hopes of peaceful exchange.

La Harpe sent the expedition's geographer, Gaston, Sieur du Rivage, up the Red River. It is probably impossible to trace du Rivage's exact route, but it is apparent he traveled west and north, perhaps reaching the Canadian River. After his return, la Harpe with nine men, including du Rivage, and twenty-two horses loaded with trade goods, set off to visit a Wichita village to the northwest. La Harpe encountered, or at least heard accounts of, nine tribes that lived along the rivers including the Comanche, Wichita, and Kiowa Apaches. After traveling for twenty-three days the group reached a large village of some six thousand people, which George H. Odell has identified through archaeological research as located about thirteen miles south of Tulsa, Oklahoma, near the Arkansas River.[2] The enormous village seems to have served as a trade center for various related tribes. La Harpe was the first French trader to reach the Wichita and Apache Indians and the first to enter what would become the state of Oklahoma. La Harpe, drawing upon du Rivage's report and his own observations, recorded information about the culture of the various tribes, information still of value to anthropologists today. The Red River expedition, however, had shown la Harpe that it was impractical to establish a settlement on the Red River, at least during that time. Upon returning, he traveled briefly to France but soon returned to Louisiana where he was given a new assignment.

In 1685, René-Robert Cavelier, Sieur de La Salle, sought to establish a colony near the mouth of the Mississippi River. Although

2. George H. Odell, *La Harpe's Post: A Tale of French-Witchita Contact on the Eastern Plains* (University of Alabama Press, 2002), 15.

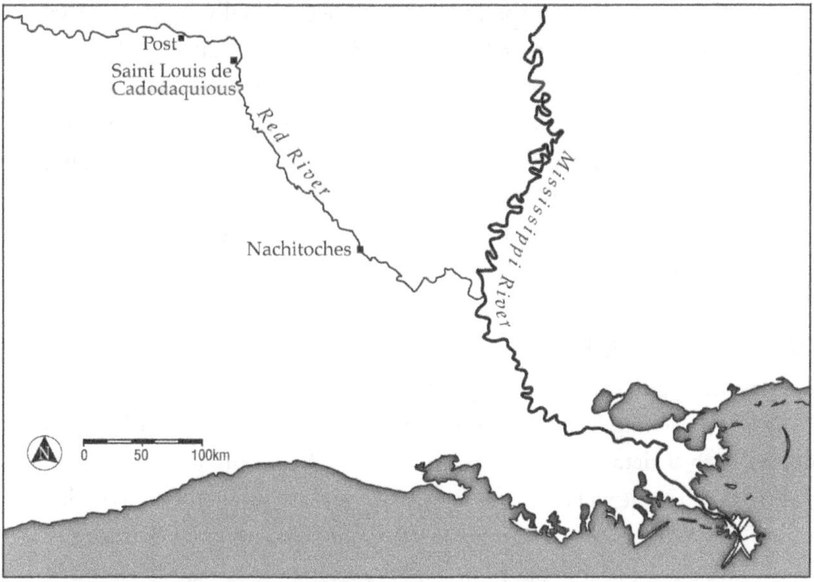

The location of Saint Louis de Cadodaquious.

La Salle had been to the mouth of the Mississippi on an earlier expedition, he apparently did not realize that the Mississippi River entered the sea at the end of a long peninsula. Elsewhere in North America, rivers joined the sea at the end of deep bays. La Salle sailed past the true mouth of the Mississippi and continued west until he entered Matagorda Bay in Texas, far west of the Mississippi River. His attempt to colonize the area was a disaster. Colonists died in great numbers and Indians killed the final remnant. La Salle was murdered by his own men. When the colony collapsed, only a few who had been exploring with La Salle managed to escape. Traces of La Salle's colony had, of course, been completely effaced long before la Harpe set out. The French, however, did not forget La Salle's failed colony, so now la Harpe was commissioned to renew La Salle's claim.

The Spanish were better acquainted than the French with the Gulf Coast, particularly the south and western sections. The northern coast, where the French were principally active, consisted largely of stretches of dull swamps interrupted occasionally by deep bays and enlivened only by terrifying thunderstorms that could easily blow a ship onto the shore if it sailed too close to the coast. It is no wonder that la Harpe accidentally landed at Galveston Bay rather than Matagorda Bay. La Harpe attempted to form a colony there, but the Indians proved hostile, and he was forced to withdraw.

La Harpe soon received a new project, best exemplified in Governor Bienvilles's own orders:

We, Jean-Baptiste de Bienville, Knight of the military order of Saint Louis, Commanding general for the King in the province of Louisiana.

It is ordered that Mr. la Harpe, Commander of the Bay of Saint Bernard, depart with a detachment of sixteen soldiers from this garrison to the Arkansas, where he will remain as long as necessary to raise provisions for his troops, and order on our authority Mr. de Francome, ensign of the garrison of the said place, to accompany him on his exploration, serving as second to him; after that the said Mr. la Harpe shall depart from here to go up the branches of the Arkansas River as high as he can, for discovering the quality of the land, the tribes that inhabit their borders, with whom he shall enter an alliance, making for us the presents that he shall judge to be necessary; he shall keep an exact journal of all that he finds on the way; he shall record the course of the rivers, their rapidity, width and depth, the quality of the timber and rocks, there should be ores, and shall bring back as much native material as he can. If he should meet by chance Spaniards, who might wish to settle upon this river, he shall pose them, informing them that we made the discovery these quarters before them; that, besides, these rivers, flowing into the Mississippi, are dependents of the government of this province. After the said Mr. La Harpe shall have executed all the above, so that nothing remains to be desired, he shall return as promptly as he can, after having left, in passing, Mr. de Francome at his post. In testimony whereof we have signed the present order and had affixed the seal of our arms.

At Fort Louis, December 10, 1721
Signed: De Bienville.[3]

3. Marc de Villiers du Terrage and Paul Rivet, *Les indiens du Texas et les expeditions françaises de 1720 et 1721 à la "Baie Sant-Bernard"* (Au siege de la Société, 1919), 423.

By late February 1722, la Harpe arrived at the Arkansas Post,[4] where he loaded supplies for forty-five days. La Harpe's expedition totaled twenty-three people, including himself, Ensign de Francome and fifteen soldiers, and several servants and slaves. What today is called the Arkansas River was known to la Harpe as the Zautoouys, a French corruption of the name Uzutiuhi, the name of a subgroup of the Quapaw Indians who had a village on the southern part of the river along with the French of the Arkansas Post. La Harpe attempted to trade for a dugout canoe, which he referred to as a pirogue. The Indians did not want to yield one of their canoes, so la Harpe attempted to seize one, almost provoking violence. Eventually, he had his men make their own pirogue, which took five days.

La Harpe was enthusiastic about the country through which they were passing on the river, and by April 7 they reached the future site of Little Rock. Contrary to some assertions, la Harpe did make brief mention of a small rock formation on the south bank of the river. He wrote that the point, simply called "the Rock" by the Indians, occurred about twenty day's journey upstream traveling by land.[5] The outcropping marked the beginning of the Ouachita Mountains and the foothills of the Ozarks, the name of which is a corruption of the French *Aux Arcs*, marking a convergence of trails to St. Louis and Santa Fe.

On April 9, they reached a natural feature that la Harpe described vividly:

> The 9th, having advanced a league, we found rocks sticking out of the ground, and have reached a league above the rock, which is on the right of the river; we named it the French Rock. It is a bluff of mountainous rock, which forms three very steep peaks, suitable for making lime; it could be 130 feet perpendicular. There are beyond some oaks, walnuts, and pines. One finds there a stone which has a relationship to marble, being very much like jasper; but it is as hard as flint; there are also several quarries of slate, but they are

4. For the Arkansas Post, Morris S. Arnold, *Colonial Arkansas 1686–1804* (University of Arkansas Press, 1991).
5. La Harpe, "Exploration of the Arkansas River," 347, 356.

not so convenient to work as that which we found at a league below; there are quarries of the most beautiful slate that one may be able to see, very fine, rising through shells, and of so great abundance that they would furnish all the colony. There is also at this rock very beautiful black stones suitable for construction purposes; they are hewn by nature and of all sizes. We climbed up this mountain and engraved on a tree upon the top the coat of arms of the King. We perceived to the westward several mountains and beautiful country. At the foot of this rock, there is a waterfall which forms a very pleasant basin, whose water is very clear and fresh.[6]

La Harpe continued upstream about twenty-five leagues, or seventy-five miles, until April 17, but then decided to turn back. Many of the men were ill, and provisions were almost exhausted, although hunting continued to be good. Before returning downriver, however, la Harpe led the men on an exploration by foot, but it soon became apparent that it was too exhausting for the men. The return downstream predictably went quicker.

Jean-François-Benjamin Dumont de Montigny participated in Bernard de la Harpe's exploration up the Arkansas River. In 1747, long after departing from Louisiana, Dumont wrote his memoire, including a fully fictious account of la Harpe's expedition:

On the second of February, there arrived at the fort the Sr. de la Harpe, captain commandant, who had received orders from the Company of the Indies to go discover, or rather to look for, a large topaz boulder [the French word is *rocher*: rock or boulder] that some flatterers had told them would be found along the river named the Zotoouis or Arkansas, for Indians who lived some sixty leagues from our concession [Dumont at this time was stationed on the Yazoo River]. He [i.e., la Harpe] also had orders to survey the river and to make an accurate journal of his travels and what he found there. . . . We all departed together, twenty-two people, that is, all going (or so they hoped) to make a quick fortune by taking possession of a topaz rock. How

6. Ralph A. Smith, Benard De La Harp,"Exploration of the Arkansas River by Benard De La Harpe, 1721-1722: Extracts from His Journal and Instructions," *The Arkansas Historical Quarterly*, Vol. 10, No. 4 (Winter, 1951), 357.

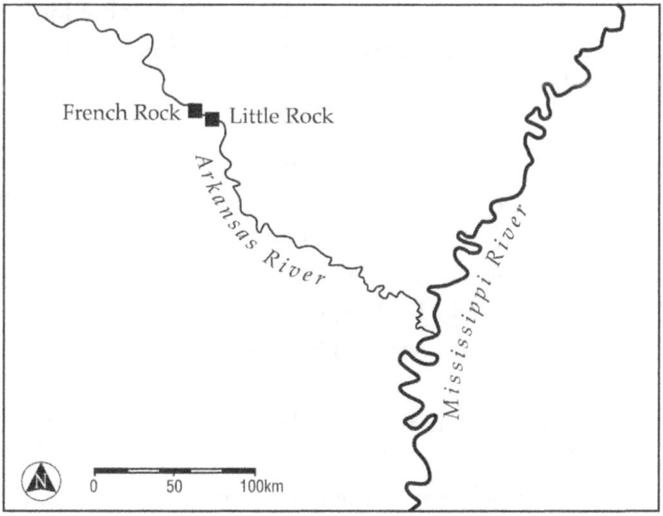

The locations of French Rock and Little Rock.

easily greed can motivate our actions, and how easily we will believe in the frauds and flattering imaginings that may be proposed to us. . . . We ascended this river for 375 leagues, though the route corrected to north and south was only 120 leagues. As we were unable to find enough water to float our boats, we were forced to travel by land for 142 leagues. When food began to run out and discontent was mounting among the detachment, we were forced to return to our pirogues and retrace our path down the river, toward the French forts among the Arkansas Indians, without being able to find the topaz boulder, which did not exist—or, if it did, existed only in the minds of some dreamer, who nonetheless had convinced the directors of the Company of the Indies. These gentlemen had sent along with us a sort of map showing the place where this precious rock was supposed to be. I do not know if it had been made a long time earlier, but the river we traveled on was nothing like the map we had been sent.[7]

7. For Dumont's original text see "François-Benjamin Dumont de Montigny," in *Regards sur le monde atlantique: 1715–1747*, ed. Denis Vaugeois (Septentrion, 2008), 154–57; for the English version see François-Benjamin Dumont de Montigny, *The Memoir of Lieutenant Dumont, 1715–1747: A Sojourner in the French Atlantic*, trans. and ed. Gordon M. Sayre and ed. Carla Zecher (University of North Carolina Press, 2012): 157–58.

Dumont also mentioned the search for the topaz boulder on the Arkansas River in a labored poem not reckoned among the gems of French Enlightenment literature:

> In the year one thousand seven hundred and twenty-two, he [Bienville] made a convoy on this tributary river. And I certainly have the right to discuss it authoritatively. I, the author of this composition, went there with twenty-two men to make this wonderful journey. We were commanded, in this detachment, by Sieur de La Harpe, appointed Commandant, to go, supposedly, to make the discovery of a boulder of topaz.[8]

Dumont's memoir, as rewritten by the Abbé Jean-Baptiste Le Mascrier, was published as *Mémoires historique sur La Louisiane.*[9] The Abbé Le Mascrier felt free in the manner of many eighteenth-century editors to change the author's words, omitting, rewriting, and interpolating to improve the work, at least in his own eyes. Le Mascrier's version often bears little resemblance to Dumont's original text. Among the changes, Le Mascrier's version claims that rather than topaz, the French explorers hoped to find an emerald boulder.[10]

La Harpe's own account of the Arkansas River expedition, *Journal Historique de l' Etablissement des Français à la Louisiane*, was apparently written about the time of his departure from Louisiana in 1723 but not published until 1831. La Harpe contradicted Dumont's account in almost every particular.[11] He stated that the directors of the Compagnie des Indes were against the Arkansas River expedition, believ-

8. Marc de Villiers du Terrage,"L'établissement de la province de Louisiane. Poème inédit de Dumont de Montigny," *Journal de la Société des Américanistes* 11 (1919): 37–38.
9. Abbé Jean-Baptiste Le Mascrier, *Mémoires historique sur La Louisiane* (Cl. J. B. Bauche, 1753).
10. François-Benjamin Dumont de Montigny, *Memoires historiques sur la Louisiane*, composed by Jean-Baptiste Le Mascrier (Chez Cl. J. B. Bauche, 1753) 2: 69–71.
11. The original publication of the journal is *Journal Historique de l' Etablissement des Français à la Louisiane* (A.-L. Boimare, 1831), which makes no attribution to an author. The modern consensus is that the journal is the work of la Harpe. A modern translation is Jean-Baptiste Bénard de La Harpe, *The Historical Journal of the Establishment of the French in Louisiana*, trans. Joan Cain and Virginia Koenig, ed. and annot. Glenn R. Conrad (University of Southwestern Louisiana, 1971).

ing it useless, but Bienville, the governor of Louisiana, took it upon himself to approve the expedition and appointed la Harpe commander. Bienville's orders contain no mention of topaz or emeralds, but merely the standard phrase indicating that should la Harpe find mines, he should bring back as many samples as possible.[12]

La Harpe also contradicted Dumont's account of exploration on the river. Dumont claimed the expedition covered 517 leagues, about 1,550 miles, while la Harpe, leader of the expedition, claimed they covered a total of only 127.5 leagues, about 380 miles. La Harpe certainly had no reason to minimize his diligence and accomplishment.

La Harpe made careful records of unusual rocks and minerals in his account of the Arkansas River expedition. He never mentioned topaz, emeralds, or other precious gems. Indeed, in his survey of the resources of French Louisiana, broadly defined, near the end of the *Journal Historique*, La Harpe made no mention of precious stones. He stated no one had yet found gold or significant silver deposits and mentioned only lead and small finds of copper.[13] Dumont's tale about an emerald boulder evidently annoyed la Harpe, who in 1763 wrote to César Gabriel de Choiseul, duc de Praslin, minister for foreign affairs, protesting that he was not looking for an emerald boulder during the exploration on the Arkansas and that his orders mentioned no jewels at all.[14]

Upon returning from the Arkansas expedition, la Harpe was given another task, returning Pensacola to the Spanish. It had been captured by the French during the War of the Quadruple Alliance, and now according to the treaty that ended the confrontation, it was to be returned. La Harpe delt with the exchange efficiently to everyone's satisfaction and returned the French garrison to Louisiana.

After returning from the expedition on the Arkansas River, la Harpe maintained that his adventures in Louisiana had seriously impaired his health. He left Louisiana for the last time in 1723,

12. La Harpe, *Journal historique*, 282–84.

13. Ibid., 366.

14. Archives Nationales, Inventaire des Archives Coloniales: C12B.1 (August 8, 1763).

returning to France and settling in his hometown of Saint-Malo, where he resided until his death in 1765.

CHAPTER FOUR

A FAMILY OF EXPLORERS

Pierre Gaultier de Varennes et de La Vérendrye and Sons

(1685–1749)

PIERRE GAULTIER DE VARENNES ET DE LA VÉRENDRYE was born on November 17, 1685, at Trois-Rivières in New France (French Canada). His family were landowners and more prosperous than average, but not truly members of the aristocracy. At one point, his father, René Gaultier de Varennes, served as governor of the town, and additionally he was active in the fur trade. Pierre was the last of nine children, and his father's fourth son.[1]

Young Pierre received a few years of education from the Jesuits and then joined the army as a cadet, hoping for eventual promotion

1. Pierre Gaultier de Varennes et de La Vérendrye and his sons have been well-known to scholars since the 1850s, although the accomplishments of the La Vérendrye family were largely ignored or discounted during their own lifetimes and subsequently. Pierre

to the status of an officer. He was only twelve years old at the time, the youngest age permissible. At the age of nineteen, during Queen Anne's War (1702–1713), he took part in the 1704 French and Indian raid on Deerfield, Massachusetts.[2] The raid killed forty-seven

Margry is responsible for the discovery and initial publication of the records of the La Vérendrye family and the first appreciation of their achievements: Pierre Margry, ed., "Esquisses de l' histoire des colonies françaises—Las Varennes de la Vérendrye. D' apres les documents inédits tires des archives des divers départements de l' état," *Moniteur Universel*, no. 258 (September 14, 1852): 1408–10; no. 258 (September 14, 1852): 1408–1410, and no. 360 (November 1, 1852): 1772–74. Lawrence J. Burpee remains the basic edition of materials about the La Vérendrye family: Lawrence J. Burpee, ed., *Journals and Letters of Pierre Gaultier de Varennes de la Vérendry and His Sons*, Publications of the Champlain Society, vol. 16 (Ballentyne Press, 1927). Orin G. Libby is notable for the argument that La Vérendrye did not reach the Mandan villages but rather visited the Hidatsa: Orin G. Libby, "La Vérendrye's Visit to the Mandans in 1738–39," *State Historical Society of North Dakota Collections* 2 (1908): 502–8; "Some Vérendrye Enigmas," *Mississippi Valley Historical Review* 3 (1916): 143–160; Introduction to "The Journal of La Vérendrye, 1738–30," ed. Henry E. Haxo, *North Dakota Historical Quarterly* 8 (1941): 229–324. G. Hubert Smith's research has effectively refuted Libby's hypothesis: G. Hubert Smith, *The Explorations of the La Vérendryes in the Northern Plains, 1738–43*, ed. W. Raymond Wood (University of Nebraska Press, 1980). Other, more modern works include Arthur Edward Jones, S. J., ed., *The Aulneau Collection 1734–1745* (Archives of St. Mary's College, 1893); Frédéric de Kastner, *Les Vérendrye père et fils, Dufrost de La Jemeraye et la découver te du Nord-ouest* (La Cie d' imprimerie commerciale, 1904); Doane Robinson, "La Veremdrye's Farthest West," Proceedings of the State Historical Society of Wisconsin, 1914 (1913): 146–50; Nellis Maynard Crouse, *La Verendrye, Fur Trader and Explorer* (Kennitak Press, 1956); Russell Reid, "Vérendrye's Journey to North Dakota in 1738," *North Dakota History* 32, no. 2 (April 1965): 117–29; Martin Kavanagh, *La Vérendrye, His Life and Times: A Biography and a Social Study of a Folklore Figure, Soldier, Fur Trader, Explorer* (M. Kavanagh, 1967); Antoine Champagne, *Nouvelles études sur les La Vérendrye de la poste de l' Ouest* (Presses de l' Université Laval, 1971); Ronald Syme and Richard Cuffari, *Fur Trader of the North: The Story of Pierre de la Veremdrye* (Morrow, 1973); George Hubert Smith, ed. W. Raymond Wood, *The Explorations of the La Vérendryes in the Northern Plains, 1738–43* (University of Nebraska Press, 1980).

2. For the Deerfield raid see, John Williams, *The Redeemed Captive, Returning to Zion: or, The Captivity and Deliverance of Rev. John Williams of Deerfield* (Phillips, 1707); *Marcel Fournier. De la Nouvelle Angleterre à la Nouvelle France - L' histoire des captifs anglo-américains au Canada entre 1675 et 1760* (Société Généalogique Canadienne-Française, 1992); Evan Haefeli and Kevin Sweeney, *Captors and Captives: The 1704 French and Indian Raid on Deerfield* (University of Massachusetts Press, 2003); Caitlyn J. Remmes, *Somewhere Between Exploitation and Partnership: English and Native Alliances Surrounding the Raids on Deerfield and King William's War* (University of Massachusetts, 2016).

English colonists, burned part of the town, and took 112 captives nearly three hundred miles away. Some died on the journey and others were killed if unable to keep up. Some of the captives were adopted into the Mohawk tribe to replace tribal members who had been killed in the war, and they thoroughly assimilated into the tribe. The English and their Indian allies also made similar raids on French villages during the war. La Vérendrye also took part in the unsuccessful French attack on the English settlement of St. John's in Newfoundland, and the subsequent burning of English fishing villages.[3]

La Vérendrye was appointed ensign, the lowest rank of officer, in the Bretagne Regiment of grenadiers then serving in Flanders. In 1707, he sailed to join the regiment in Europe and served there during the War of the Spanish Succession (1701–1714). There he took part in the famous Battle of Malplaquet, fought in 1709 within the province of Hainaut in France. An alliance of forces commanded by John Churchill, Duke of Marlborough, opposed the French army under the Duke de Villars. The allies suffered heavy casualties but eked out a slight tactical victory, while the French were able to withdraw in good order and prevented further allied advances. La Vérendrye was repeatedly wounded during the battle, reported to have been shot once and received eight saber cuts. He collapsed on the battlefield and was left for dead. He recovered, was released in 1710, and then promoted to lieutenant. Seeing no hope of further promotion, he left the army. The higher ranks of the French army were essentially reserved for the aristocracy and those alone who had influence among important officials in the army and court. La Vérendrye returned to New France in 1711.

1n 1712, La Vérendrye married Marie-Ann du Sable, daughter of Louis Dandonneau du Sable, Sieur de l' Ile du Pas. A son, Jean-Baptiste, was born on September 5, 1713, and a second son, Pierre, was born on December 26, 1714. A third son, François, was born on

3. For the raid on St. John's in Newfoundland see, René Baudry, "Auger De Subercase, Daniel D'," in *Dictionary of Canadian Biography*, vol. 2, University of Toronto/Université Laval, 2003, accessed May 21, 2023, http://www.biographi.ca/en/bio/auger_de_subercase _ daniel_d_2E.html.

December 22, 1715, and a fourth son, Louis-Joseph, was born on November 9, 1717. All four sons would play significant roles in their father's western explorations. A nephew, Christophe Dufrot, Sieur de la Jémeraye, baptized December 17, 1708, also served with La Vérendrye and may have even visited the Fox, Winnebago, and Sioux (Dakota) before La Vérendrye, or at least contemporaneously with La Vérendrye's first ventures to the west.

Other than having children, little is known of La Vérendrye's activities in the years immediately after leaving the army, except that he ran a trading post called La Gabelle (The Tax) on the Saint-Maurice River that runs through Trois-Rivières. The post sought to trade with Indians before they got to the town itself.

A frequent concern in the eighteenth century was to discover a way to the "Western Sea" (i.e., the Pacific Ocean). Early geographic theory held that in the West a vast gulf existed, something like Hudson's Bay to the north, and when discovered it would offer a fast and convenient passage to China and lucrative trade. La Vérendrye and his sons would eventually be able to prove that this theory was incorrect. Indian tribes had intimate knowledge of the territory they inhabited, but distant areas were matters of rumor and speculation. It is doubtful that La Vérendrye ever fully realized this, and he eagerly questioned Indians of various tribes and even had them prepare maps that proved to be of dubious reliability. Another vital interest was competition with the English who traded for furs at Hudson's Bay. Throughout the eighteenth century, rivalry between the British and French repeatedly led to war, and even in times of peace the economic competition was intense and sometimes violent.

In 1727, La Vérendrye was appointed commandant of the posts in the North. He was then forty-two years old, a substantial age in the eighteenth century. While he would continue exploring for many years, he would come to rely increasingly on his sons. In 1731, La Vérendrye made his first trip into the Northwest, and during that same year he sent his nephew La Jémeraye to establish Fort St. Pierre on Rainy Lake, the first of a series of trading posts.

Soon after La Vérendrye was appointed commandant of the northern and western posts, he began to plan explorations to the

West. In 1730, he submitted a report to the governor, Charles de la Boische, Marquis de Beauharnois, consisting of information about the West that he had gathered from Indians, particularly the Cree who ranged widely. The stories told by the Indians were often a mixture of reliable material about nearby areas with which they were fully acquainted and fantasies about distant ones. La Vérendrye, of course, was most interested in reports of a great river that flowed to the west. In 1731, he, along with his three eldest sons, embarked on their first westward expedition. La Vérendrye went from Fort Kamanistikwia, on the shore of Lake Superior north of Grand Portage, to Fort St. Pierre on Rainy Lake, and from there to Lake of the Woods where he was present at the construction of Fort St. Charles. La Vérendrye sent La Jémeraye to Governor Beauharnois with a map made on this expedition that bore new and important information. It correctly showed Lake Winnipeg's outlet to Hudson's Bay rather than to the Pacific as previously assumed, and it introduced a western tribe with whom the French had not previously been acquainted, the Ouachipouennes or "Sioux [Dakota] who go underground," so called because of their earth lodges. The Cree and Assiniboin were often at war with the Ouachipouennes. Throughout the early 1730s, La Vérendrye continued to gather information about the West, primarily from the Cree and Assiniboin.

In 1734, La Vérendrye established Fort Maurepas I on the Red River by the south shore of Lake Winnipeg. This was the first of several Forts with the same name. The fort was subsequently moved somewhat north and east along the shore of the lake. The forts were named for Jean-Frédéric Phélypeaux, Count de Maurepas, adviser to the king and minister of the marines in charge of French colonies. In 1738, La Vérendrye established Fort la Reine on the Assiniboine River, and about that time Fort Maurepas was abandoned and replaced by Fort Rouge at the site of modern Winnipeg. Forts Dauphin and the first Fort Bourbon followed probably in 1741. Fort Dauphin was located on the small Dauphin Lake south of Lake Winnipegosis, and the first Fort Bourbon was built on the west end of Cedar Lake, north of Lake Winnipegosis. Fort Bourbon was later relocated to northern Lake Winnipegosis.

La Vérendrye was under increasing pressure from the government to find the fabled river running to the west and presumably reaching the Pacific. Beauharnois assured Maurepas that La Vérendrye had only the best of intentions, but exploration was expensive and detracted from the business of fur trading on which La Vérendrye and his family depended. Beauharnois permitted La Vérendrye to rent his posts to others for a period of three years which enabled him to pursue the discovery of the river. So in June 1735, La Vérendrye set out for the West. He was accompanied by his youngest son, who had been trained in mathematics and drawing, which enabled him to make accurate maps. The pair wintered at Fort St. Charles at Lake of the Woods. In 1736, La Jémeraye, a nephew, died, and the Sioux (Dakota) killed Jean-Baptiste, La Vérendrye's second son, along with a priest, Jean-Pierre Aulneau, S.J., and nineteen voyageurs on Lake of the Woods. These deaths deeply affected La Vérendrye, scared the men who worked for him, and curtailed further exploration at the time. By September he had recovered the bodies of his son, the priest, and skulls of the voyageurs. It had proved impractical to move all twenty-one corpses, and by taking only the skulls, at least some portion of them would rest in consecrated ground. La Vérendrye had them interred by the chapel at Fort St. Charles.

In 1737, La Vérendrye and his son, while at Lake of the Woods, produced a new map based largely on information chiefly from the Assiniboin, which showed that the sought-after river flowed south rather than west, and that it led to Spanish territory. The map also incorporated indications of the mountain range to the west, one that neither La Vérendrye nor his sons had seen, but still the first indication of the Rocky Mountains. The Assiniboin also indicated that a river arising in these mountains did flow westward. The exploration that began in 1736 concluded without La Vérendrye having progressed farther west than Fort Maurepas on the Red River, a disappointment to both him and Governor Beauharnois.

La Vérendrye's activities in 1738 are known from one document, often incorrectly referred to as a "journal." The document is a letter addressed to the Marquis de Beauharnois, the governor of New

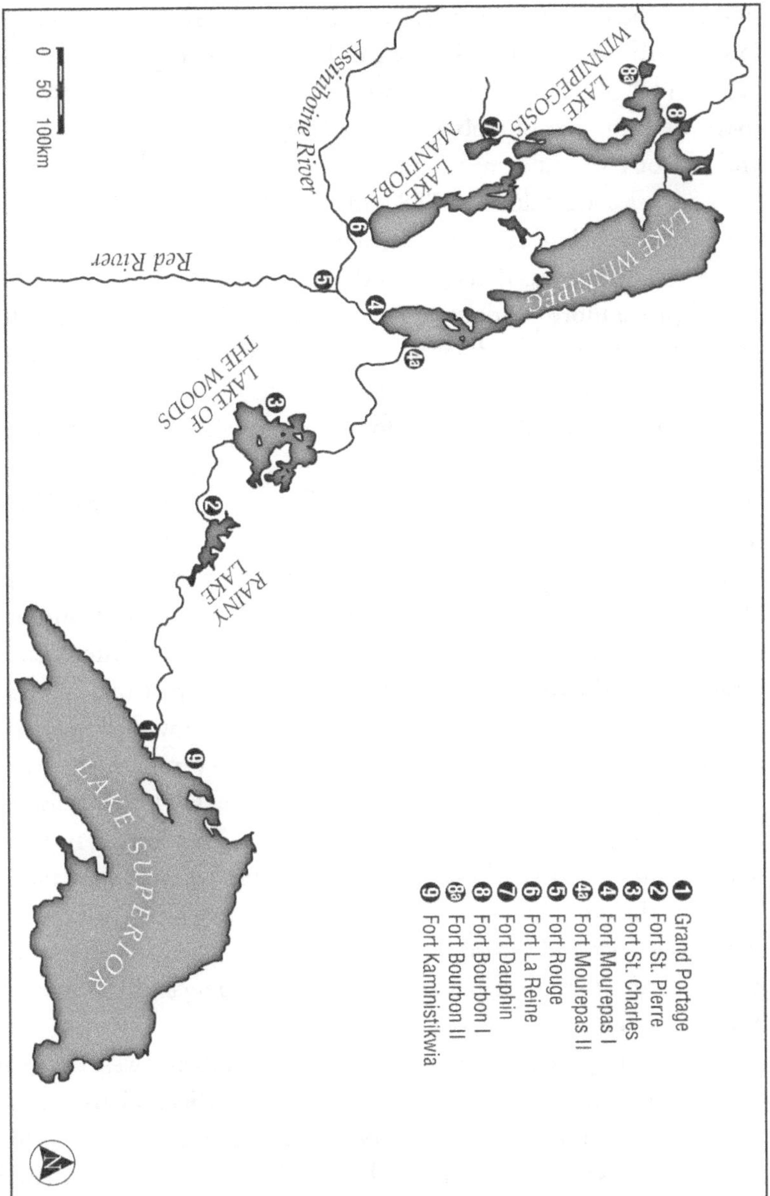

Forts associated with the La Vérendrye expeditions. Grand Portage was founded before the La Vérendrye forts. The French were active in the areas during the seventeenth century. Fort Kaministikwia was also founded before the La Vérendrye forts, but often served as the beginning of La Vérendrye's expeditions.

France. The original seems lost, and there appears to be no copy found within any archive in France. The existing copy, twenty-two pages in length, is now in the public archives of Canada. However, there are a number of ambiguities and uncertainties in the account, and various recent commentators have endeavored to trace La Vérendrye's course during 1738 and 1739. While the evidence does not permit absolute certainty, the most likely course can be traced.

La Vérendrye was determined that his new explorations in 1738 would prove more productive than those of 1736, blighted by the sad deaths of his son and nephew. He reached Fort Kamanisttikwia on August 5 and soon departed for Fort St. Pierre on Rainy Lake. La Vérendrye left orders behind for Charles Nolan, Sieur de la Marque, a trade associate, to follow. By the end of August, La Vérendrye and his party were at Fort St. Charles at Lake of the Woods. There he left his youngest son as commandant and departed after a meeting with Indians on September 11. They proceeded to the southern end of Lake Winnipeg, where La Vérendrye had the first Fort Maurepas constructed. From there they went to the confluence of the Assiniboine and Red Rivers on September 24. The summer of 1738 was exceptionally hot and dry. The Assiniboine River was so low that canoes could not be used without danger of severe damage from grounding or encountering barely submerged rocks. This encouraged La Vérendrye and his sons to travel by land. They first traveled a westward parallel to the river, establishing Fort La Reine, the name honoring the queen. La Marque finally caught up with La Vérendrye at the new fort and informing him that all was well stated that he had erected a fort, Fort Rouge, near the confluence of the Assiniboine and Red Rivers.

La Vérendrye and the party next traveled south and west to reach villages on what is now known as the Missouri River where a tribe whose name La Vérendrye understood as "Mantanne," now more generally known as the Mandans, had settled. La Vérendrye visited two of the Mantanne fortresses that impressed him as well-constructed and strong. He also remarked on their excellent upkeep and neatness. The Missouri River seemed to be the long-sought "River of the West," though, of course, it would eventually prove not to flow

The La Vérendrye brothers in sight of the western mountains by Charles Jefferys, ca. 1915. (*New York Public Library*)

to the Pacific. The Mantanne guided Louis-Joseph and Nolan to another large river flowing southwest. The Mantanne indicated that the river downstream turned more to the west, although native information about geography beyond the immediate area often proved less than reliable.

The season was now so far advanced that there was no opportunity for further exploration, so La Vérendrye decided to return to Fort La Reine, leaving behind two Frenchmen to learn the Mantanne language. At the beginning of the return in early December, La Vérendrye fell ill. They reached La Reine on February 10, 1739. La Vérendrye was alive, but exhausted. He was now fifty-three years old, and life on the frontier had begun to take a toll. Henceforth, his sons would assume the burden of exploration.

In 1742, François de La Vérendrye, known as the Chevalier,[4] accompanied by his brother, Louis-Joseph, set out on a new explo-

4. There is some debate about which of the brothers was known as the Chevalier. The consensus is that François was so designated.

ration that would take them farther west than their father's journeys. The expedition is known through a letter, again often incorrectly referred to as a "journal," written to Beauharnois. It lacks date and place of composition, and it appears that François composed it from memory. There is no indication that the explorers kept a daily journal of any sort. The original appears not to have been preserved, but a copy is now in the French Service Hydographiqie.[5] Again, there is controversy over exactly where they traveled, but a consensus prevails.

Leaving from Fort La Reine, the brothers and their party traveled first to the west, roughly paralleling the Assiniboine River, then turning south to the Mandan villages. From there they proceeded westward, then south and southwest. They encountered a variety of plains tribes, but it is difficult to equate the generic names given in the report to the names of historic tribes in the areas in which they traveled. The "Gens des Chevaux" or Horse People may be the Cheyenne,[6] while the "Gens de la Belle Rivère," People of the Beautiful River, may be another group of the Cheyenne. The dreadful "Gens de Serpent," People of the Serpent, much feared by other tribes, were probably the Shoshone, and the "Gens de la Flêche Collêe," People of the Glued Arrow, may have been some group of the Sioux (Dakota). The "Gens de l' Arc," People of the Bow, may have been a group of western Sioux (Dakota) or perhaps the Pawnee, and the "Gens de la Petite Cerise," People of the Small Cherry, may have been the Arikaras. These identifications are probable, but not certain. Tribal structures were unstable as groups combined or broke apart, and tribes recognized in the nineteenth century may or may not have existed as units in the first half of the eighteenth century.

At the most southern and western extent of their exploration, the brothers may have been able to see the Big Horn range of mountains. At this point they moved a little north and then east, passing close to the Black Hills and then reaching the Missouri River, which they followed to the northwest until in the vicinity of modern Pierre,

5. A copy is preserved and held within the French Service Hydographique.
6. For these identifications see Smith, *Explorations*, 117–23 and Francis Parkman, *A Half-Century of Conflict*, vol. 2. (Little, Brown, and Co., 1897), 43.

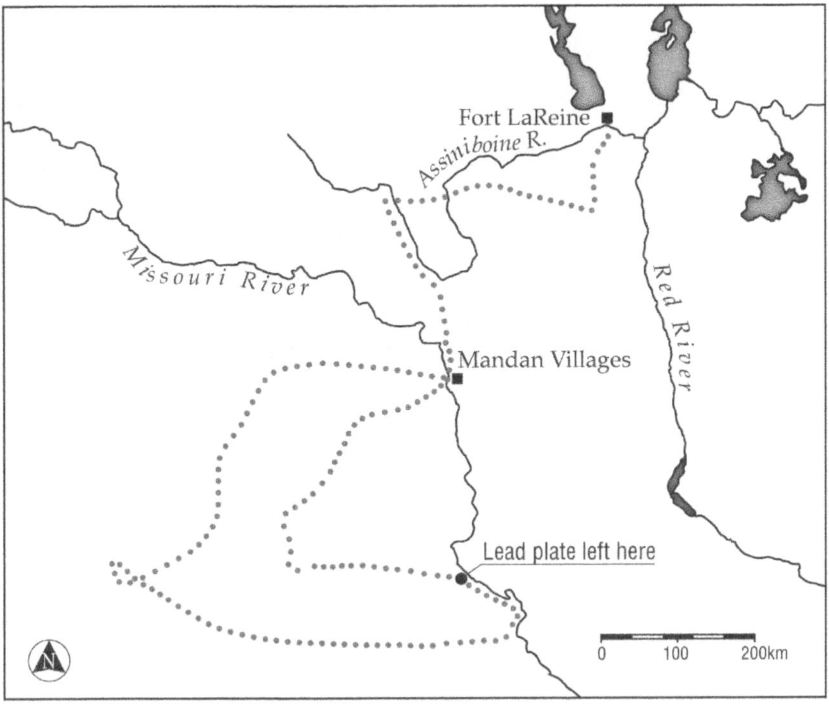

The location of the Vérendrye lead plate.

South Dakota, where they buried a "lead tablet" that was discovered by school children in 1913. The front of the tablet, or plate, has a Latin message which may be translated as follows: "In the twenty-sixth year of the reign of Louis XV, the Marquis de Beauharnois being the most illustrious viceregent. 1741. Pierre Gaultier de La Verendrye deposited." Scratched into the reverse of this tablet, largely abbreviated, is the following: "Placed by the Che(valier) de La V(erendre) et de Lo(uis) Jos(eph) Louis La Londette A Miotte March 30, 1743."

At this point they seem to have moved west into the plain, and then finally determining it was time to return, they headed north and northeast to the Mandan villages.

The two brothers and their companions had explored a vast section of the Great Plains and claimed the area for the king of France,

The Vérendrye lead plate discovered in 1913. (*South Dakota Historical Society*)

but their discoveries were dismissed as largely irrelevant. The Great Plains did not produce the sought after beaver skins that brought a good price in Europe, and buffalo skins were in low demand and heavy to transport. This was the last great exploration by the La Vérendrye family, a success but unappreciated.

In 1744, La Vérendrye was removed as commandant of the northern and western posts. He and his family had explored widely and claimed much land in the name of the French king, but they had failed to discover the fabled way to the Pacific and had discovered no substantial new trade resources. His successor lasted less than two years in office; La Vérendrye was reappointed. He was honored by promotion to captain and eventually granted the Grand

Cross of the Order of Saint-Louis, a much-coveted award, but La Vérendrye had gone heavily into debt to finance his explorations, and the royal French government did nothing substantial to recompense him. La Vérendrye died early in December of 1749, heavily in debt and ignored except for empty honors.

It was not until the middle of the nineteenth century that the scope of these discoveries by La Vérendrye and his sons began to be appreciated.

CHAPTER FIVE

ACROSS THE PLAINS TO SANTA FE

Pierre Antoine Mallet and Paul Mallet

(ca. 1704–ca. 1750/ca. 1706–ca.1753)

Pierre Antoine Mallet was born about 1704 and his brother Paul about two years later in Montreal to Pierre Mallet and Madelaine Tuvée Du Fresne.[1] They received the typical education of frontier boys, short on formal education but long on hard work and practical training.

About 1734, the two moved to Kaskaskia in the Illinois Country. Kaskaskia was the largest settlement in the Midwest until the rise of St. Louis. In the 1880s, the Mississippi River changed course and eventually washed Kaskaskia entirely away because the town was established on unconsolidated sedimentary soil. What is called Kaskaskia today is New Kaskaskia, dating only from the 1890s.[2]

1. Some sources claim Pierre Antoine Mallet was born in 1700.

2. David MacDonald and Raine Waters, *Kaskaskia: The Lost Capital of Illinois* (Shawnee Books, 2019).

From Kaskaskia, uncertain about the location of Santa Fe, their intended destination, the brothers and their companions proceeded to the north and west, through Nebraska and into South Dakota until friendly Indians showed them conventional trails to the Southwest. At an Omaha village in northeastern Nebraska, they traded for horses for their overland trip.

The Mallet brothers and seven companions (Phillippe Robitaille, Louis Morin, Michel Beslot called La Rose, Joseph Bellecourt, Emanuel Galien (or Gallien), Jean David known as Petit-Jean, and Louis Moreau) traveled through what would become the states of Kansas and western Oklahoma to Santa Fe. All did not go as planned. At the Smoke Hill River, a branch of what the brothers labeled the River of the Kansas, the expedition lost seven horses loaded with merchandise. Paul seems to have been the more articulate of the brothers, and it was he who probably kept the journal of their travels. In the journal it is reported that the river was deep and had a strong current. Though deprived of most of their merchandise, the brothers and their companions persisted in their determination to reach Santa Fe.[3]

The Mallets and their companions reached Santa Fe in 1739 and were welcomed there. They stayed for the winter. In 1740, they were determined to travel to New Orleans, carrying letters from the lieutenant governor of New Mexico and from a priest, both of whom encouraged trade between the French and Spanish colonies.

Copy of Certificate to seven Frenchmen at Santa Fe by General Jean Paez Hurtado, *alcalde major* and Captain of War of this capital city of Santa Fe and its jurisdiction, Lieutenant Governor and Captain General of this Kingdom of New Mexico and its provinces:

I myself certify to Captain Don Louis de Saint-Denis, who commands the fort at the mouth of the Red River, and to all other governors and captains, judges and justices of the very Christian King of France, to all military and political officers to whom this may be presented, that on the 24th of July of

3. Donald J. Blakeslee, *Along Ancient Trails: The Mallet Expedition of 1739* (University Press of Colorado, 1995), 25-27.

the past year, 1739, there arrived in this city of Santa Fe eight Frenchmen named Pierre and Paul Mallet, brothers, Phillippe Robitaille, Louis Morin, Michel Beslot, Joseph Bellecourt, and Manuel Gallien, native-born men of Canada in New France, and Jean David of Europe, who were received in my presence by Domingo de Mendoza, Lieutenant-Colonel, Governor and Lieutenant General of this realm, at the gate of the palace, where Paul Mallet entered with the governor and with Sir Santiago Reibaldo, Vicar of this realm. The governor asked them where they came from and to what purpose. Paul answered that they came from New France and that they had come with the intent to initiate a trade with the Spanish of this realm because of the intimate connection that exists between the crowns of France and Spain.

I certify that, with this understood, the lord governor sent their guns to the guards and searched for a place for the Frenchmen to stay, because he had no room at the palace. I took them into my home where I lodged them all, and, a few days later, I sent for their arms and ammunitions and for some old clothes for their use, that they had salvaged from an accident they suffered while crossing a river, where they lost nine horses laden with merchandise and their clothing, the remainder amounting to nearly nothing. According to their report, they were still intent to discover this kingdom and to open communication with the colonies of New Orleans and Canada, and disdainful of all sorts of troubles and risks from the savage nations that they might encounter, they came to see the Spanish, by whom they were well received, as they were invited by them to dine in their homes and to stay with them, while awaiting the response of the Lord Archbishop, Viceroy of Mexico, Don Juan Antonio Vizarron, which took nine months.

During this interval, the Mallet brothers, who stayed with me and dined at my table, maintained a very regular and very Christian conduct, and as they intended to return, I recommended that should they obtain a royal patent for trade with this kingdom, they should bring a certificate and passport from their governor, because without these, they would expose themselves to the confiscation of what they carried, which would be regarded as contraband.
Sincerely,
Given at Santa Fe, 30 April, 1740
Signed: Juan Paez Hurtado[4]

4. Blakeslee, *Along Ancient Trails*, 221-222.

The trade described in the letter was contrary to Spanish imperial policy, which tried to enforce a perfect mercantilist policy with its colonies. All goods were to come from manufacturers in Spain while all goods from the colonies were supposed to flow back to Spain. The problem was that manufacturers in Spain produced too few goods to satisfy colonial demand. Illegal trading took place in virtually every colony.

Paul Mallet kept a journal of the expedition, but it seems not to have survived, although there is still some hope that it will one day be discovered bound with some other journal. Fortunately, Governor Jean-Baptiste Le Moyne de Bienville, the governor of French Louisiana, had a summary prepared of the Mallet journal. The summary is not always clear and lacks detail at crucial points, but it is the best source for the Mallet expedition of 1739–1740.[5]

In 1740, their expedition continued on to New Orleans, but after leaving Santa Fe the expedition began to disintegrate. Five men had elected to accompany the Mallet brothers to New Orleans, but while on the trip, three decided to leave and return to Kaskaskia. Joseph Bellecourt, Emanuel Galien, and Jean David nicknamed "Petit-Jean," left the Mallets. The road was long and rough, but the three eventually made it back to the Illinois Country. Only Michel Beslot (or Belau), who went by the nickname "La Rose," and Phillippe Robitaille continued in the company of the Mallets, who reached New Orleans in 1740.

Soon another expedition, headed this time by Fabry de la Bruyere, set out from New Orleans to travel to Santa Fe for trade. The Mallets accompanied the expedition and seemed to have been

5. Donald J. Blakeslee, *Along Ancient Trails: The Mallet Expedition of 1739* (University Press of Colorado, 1995), 23–29; Henry Folmer, "The Mallet Expedition of 1739 through Nebraska, Kansas, and Colorado to Santa Fe," *Colorado Magazine*, 1939, 163–173; "Mallet Brothers," *Encyclopedia of the Great Plains*, accessed December 1, 2024, http://plainshumanities.unl.edu/encyclopedia/doc/egp.ea.026; "Extract of the Journal of the Expedition of the Mallet Brothers to Santa Fe, 1739–1740," accessed December 1, 2024, www.americanjourneys.org/aj-092/summary/index.asp. Governor Bienville sent a summary of the journal to Paris. A copy of the document has survived (AN, Col. F3 24: 387-391vo; photocopy in Library of Congress, Manuscript Division).

in constant conflict with de la Bruyere over the conduct of the journey. It proved a great failure. Most of the trade goods were lost crossing the Canadian River, and the group did not get past eastern Oklahoma before turning back to New Orleans.[6] The idea of trade between the French and the Spanish at Santa Fe languished until 1750 when Pierre Antoine Mallet proposed a new expedition to the governor of Louisiana, Pierre François de Ridaud, the Marquis de Vaudrueil. The governor approved it and the expedition set forth. Seven days before the arrival at Santa Fe, Comanche Indians intercepted the expedition and thoroughly looted the explorers of the trade goods and documents, damaging much of what they did not take.[7]

A greater problem, however, was that the new governor of Santa Fe took the royal Spanish prohibition against trading with foreigners seriously. He promptly arrested Pierre Antoine Mallet who lacked proper documentation, as it had been stolen in the Comanche raid. Unfortunately, Pierre Antoine disappeared into the Spanish prison system, undoubtedly sent to the central prison in Mexico City. It is not known how long he lingered there until succumbing to death in the notoriously unhealthy jail.

Paul Mallet did not take part in the 1750 expedition. He is last heard of settling at the Arkansas Post with a wife and three daughters. There he undoubtedly farmed for a living and perhaps did a little trading with passing merchants.

6. Blakeslee's *Along Ancient Trails* (182–92) also covers the de la Bruyere expedition; Martha Royce Blaine, "French Efforts to Reach Santa Fe: Andre Fabry do la Bruyere's Voyage up the Canadian River in 1741–1742," *Louisiana History: The Journal of the Louisiana Historical Association* 20, no. 2 (Spring 1979): 133–57.

7. Blakeslee's *Along Ancient Trails* (245–48) also includes two letters concerning the 1750 expedition and an inventory of goods that survived the Comanche looting.

CHAPTER SIX

CAUGHT BETWEEN TWO POWERS

Jean-Baptiste de Couagne

(ca. 1720–1796)

The life of Jean-Baptiste de Couagne illustrates a frontiersman caught up in the conflicts between the French and British in North America. De Couagne, whose name was also written as Du Coigne among other forms, was baptized on March 3, 1720. Baptism generally took place promptly after birth. His family were merchants, and Jean-Baptiste entered the fur trade at a young age. His family sent him to the Illinois Country about 1736 as an *engagé*, an indentured employee under contract to a more experienced trader.[1]

The Kaskaskia manuscripts indicate that between 1742 and 1747, Jean-Baptiste operated independently as a trader at Vincennes

1. David MacDonald and Raine Waters, *Kaskaskia: The Lost Capital of Illinois* (Shawnee Books, 2019). 43; 180.23.

and Kaskaskia. At some point, he entered a liaison with Elisabeth-Michel Rouensa, a member of a leading family among the Kaskaskia Indians even before first European contact. The pair had a son, also named Jean-Baptiste. His last name is spelled variously in the sources, but the form "Du Coigne" is now most often used.

Jean-Baptiste Du Coigne the son was not born in 1750, despite frequent assertions that he was. In that year Father Gagnon, the parish priest of Ste. Anne's Church by Fort de Chartes baptized a child named Louis Ducoigne, not Jean-Baptiste.[2] Louis Ducoigne appears in no other document, and no baptismal record survives for Jean-Baptiste Ducoigne. Writers conclude without proof that they were the same person, and that Louis's name was changed to Jean-Baptiste. There is no baptismal record for Jean-Baptiste Ducoigne for a simple reason: his father and mother spent much of their time at Vincennes, and no Vincennes baptismal records survive from the mid-eighteenth century. Jean-Baptiste was probably born at Vincennes, and it is likely that Louis Ducoigne was a brother who died young, as did so many other children in the eighteenth century. It was Jean-Baptiste Du Coigne who grew up to become the paramount chief of the Kaskaskia Indians.[3]

Jean-Baptiste de Couagne the father did not remain long in Illinois after the birth of his son. In 1747, he was at Montreal where he contracted to go as an *engagé* to Detroit and in 1749 he was similarly employed to go to Lake of the Woods, in modern Minnesota. During the winter of 1750–1751, Jean-Baptiste de Couagne was at Fort Lydius, also known as Fort Edward, in New York. While there he associated with John Hendricks Lÿdius, to whom he may have been related by marriage. Lÿdius was probably responsible for introducing de Couagne to English authorities.

Lÿdius was a complex and questionable character. Of Belgian descent, he lived first in northern New York before moving to Montreal in 1725. There he converted from Calvinism to Roman Catholicism and prospered as an Indian trader, primarily among the Iroquois.

2. MacDonald and Waters, *Kaskaskia: The Lost Capital of Illinois*, 44; 181–182.
3. Ibid., 43–44, 66–71, 75–76.

Lÿdius was also deeply involved in the illegal but profitable trade between French Montreal and English Albany in New York. Convicted of illegal trade, he was banished from New France and sent to prison in Rochefort, France, but there he convinced authorities he was Dutch and had substantial resources in Montreal, both false. They released him, and he absconded to New York where he established a post known as both Fort Lydius and Fort Edward on the trade route between New France and New York. In 1744, France declared war on Britain. Known to the English speakers as King George's War, the conflict continued to 1748. In 1745, a French expedition burned Lÿdius's post. Lÿdius subsequently was involved in questionable land deals that alienated both the Iroquois and New York officials. He eventually moved to England, where he falsely claimed an aristocratic title. He died there in 1791.[4]

De Couagne likely had been associated with Lÿdius in the illegal trade between New France and Albany and so had escaped to English territory. In the spring of 1751, Sir William Johnson, superintendent of the northern Indians, wrote to the governor of New York seeking permission for de Couagne to engage in business within the colony. Also in 1751, the governor of New France, Jacques-Pierre de Taffanel de la Jonquière, Marquis de La Jonquière, displeased at de Couagne's activity with the English, ordered his arrest. De Couagne, of course, was far from Taffanel's grasp, although de Couagne continued to correspond with people in Montreal.

Britain and France officially went to war in 1754, but in the Midwest violence between the two nations and their allies had commenced long before that date. This left de Couagne, French but associating with the English, in a delicate position, suspected by authorities of both powers. In 1757, he and a partner were imprisoned at Albany on suspicion, but soon they appeared at liberty again, although it is not clear whether they escaped or were released. In 1758, after spending some time among the Iroquois, they were sent to the British commander in chief, James Abercromby, who personally

4. Peter N. Moogk, "Lydius, John Hendricks," *Dictionary of Canadian Biography*, vol. 4, University of Toronto/Université Laval, 2003– , accessed May 10, 2023, http://www.biographi.ca/en/bio/lydius_john_hendricks_4E.html.

questioned du Couagne. He must have given a good account of himself since the British subsequently employed him as an interpreter and secret agent operating among the Indians.[5]

Abercromby initially sent du Couagne back to the Iroquois, and he subsequently lived and served as a British agent among the Ojibwa, Potawatomi, various tribes along the Ohio River, the Iroquois, and even had a son by a Seneca woman. He was captured by the Cherokee but convinced them not only to spare him but even to adopt him into the tribe. By 1778, du Couagne was employed as the interpreter at Niagara, but his eyesight was failing, and by 1780 he had retired to Montreal, where he was still living in 1796.[6]

Du Couagne may be regarded as typical of individuals caught in the cross currents of imperial conflicts. Did he come to the realization that French efforts in North America were foredoomed? Nothing suggests du Cougne possessed that level of political foresight. More likely, fleeing from charges of illegal trading in Montreal, he simply fell in with the English and sought to make the best of the situation in which he found himself.

5. Jane E. Graham, "Couagne, Jean-Baptiste De (fl. 1720–96)," *Dictionary of Canadian Biography*, vol. 4, University of Toronto/Université Laval, 2003– , accessed May 9, 2023, http://www.biographi.ca/en/bio/couagne_jean_baptiste_de_1720_96_4E. html.
6. Ibid.

CHAPTER SEVEN

UNDER THREE FLAGS

Philippe–François de Rastel de Rocheblave

(1727–1802)

PHILIPPE-FRANÇOIS DE RASTEL DE ROCHEBLAVE was born in Savournon, Hautes-Alpes, France, on March 23, 1727. His father, Jean Joseph de Rastel was Sieur of Savournon, Chevalier, and Marquis de Rocheblave. The Rocheblave family owned a château at Ispagnac by the entrance of the *gorges du Tarn*. The earliest part of the château, which dates to the sixteenth century, is now largely in ruins, but the more recent construction remains intact and inhabited, as Rocheblave's family was quite large having twenty-one siblings.[1]

1. Geneanet. Marquerite Rose de Rastel de Rocheblave. gw.geneanet.org/wailly?lang=en&n=de+rastel+de+rocheblave&oc=0&p=marquerite+rose.

Rocheblave joined the French army and in 1745 fought in the great French victory at Fontenoy in Belgium during the War of the Austrian Succession. With the coming of peace in 1748 he, like most other officers, was placed on half pay. Later, Rocheblave served in the French West Indies. During the French and Indian War, as the Seven Years War was called in America, he served first under Charles Michel de Langlade and took part in Braddock's defeat at Monongahela in 1755. By 1760, he was serving in Illinois where he initially held the rank of lieutenant and eventually rose to the rank of captain of the French marines. He commanded the small Fort Massiac on the Ohio River briefly and then became the town commandant at Kaskaskia. There, in 1763, he married the daughter of a Kaskaskia militia leader, Marie-Michel Dufresne. With the coming of peace in 1763 he was again placed on half pay. He resigned from the French army in 1764. Many of the officers and men of the French forces returned to France, where the royal government largely ignored their legitimate claims, particularly those of the French marines. Some remained in America, Rocheblave among them.

Rocheblave initially settled in Kaskaskia where he became a merchant, but in 1766 he left Kaskaskia to cross over to the west side of the Mississippi River and enter Spanish service as commandant of the town of Sainte-Geneviève. Rocheblave served Spain conscientiously, but he clashed with the British commander at Fort de Chartres over the behavior of British soldiers and argued with don Francisco Rìu, commander of the first Spanish expeditionary force to reach Illinois. When the Spanish replaced Rocheblave as the commandant of Sainte-Geneviève, he felt insulted, and after a short time crossed back to the British side of the river. In 1772 as the English colonies grew increasingly restive, the British withdrew most of their troops from the Illinois Country. At Kaskaskia, Rocheblave became acquainted with Captain Hugh Lord, the last British commander of Illinois. In 1776, Lord and the last British troops were withdrawn from Illinois and sent east, and Lord recommended Rocheblave to fill the post of administrator.

The British expected Rocheblave to do nothing more than publish governmental decrees, preside over the court at Kaskaskia, and write

Detail from an eighteenth-century map showing the confluence of the Missouri and Mississippi Rivers, with Fort Chartres, Kaskaskia, and Ste. Genevieve to the south. (*Library of Congress*)

reports on the activities of the Spanish and Indians. He intended, however, to serve fully as the governor of the Illinois Country. He dealt effectively with a wide variety of issues, including relations with Indian tribes and the difficult problem of balancing British and French interests. It was not an easy task, as Rocheblave's own words attest:

> I was in command formerly in these parts for three years; and had not during that time to decide more than one process a week. . . . At present one is obliged every day to imprison young men who demand that if the English law if favorable to them it should be followed; on another occasion the same people will the very next day demand the old French laws which have always been followed. If I were not a little crazed already, I believe they would cause me to become entirely so.[2]

2. Rocheblave to Lieut.-Gov. Hamilton, May 8, 1777, citing *Canadian Archives*, Series Q, 14: 56, translated in Edward Gay Mason, *Philippe de Rocheblave and Rocheblave Papers*, Fergus' Historical Series, no. 84 (Fergis Printing Company, 1896), 262.

Rocheblave infuriated his superiors because he routinely exceeded the very modest sum he was allowed for expenses. He also repeatedly informed his superiors concerning the vulnerability of the Illinois Country. There were militias in each town, but they had repeatedly refused to report to earlier British commandants, and Rocheblave had no reason to believe they would obey any order he might issue. The Illinois French resented British rule. Not only were the British traditional enemies, but their administration had been inept and occasionally corrupt. Rocheblave was neither, but he bore the onus of earlier misdeeds. He did send watchers to observe the Mississippi, but there was nothing else he could do. He simply had no forces at his disposal, and his superiors ignored his pleas for any.

In 1778, George Rogers Clark sent two spies to Illinois to gather information. Their report greatly encouraged him. With only about 175 men, Clark traveled down the Ohio River to the site of the abandoned French fort of Massiac, at modern Metropolis, Illinois. From there he marched cross-country and without being observed approached Kaskaskia, the largest of the French villages and center of administration. Clark captured Kaskaskia without firing a shot and arrested Rocheblave in his quarters. Don Fernando de Leyba, the Spanish commander at St. Louis, reported Rocheblave's statement to Clark, as Rocheblave remained defiant in the face of captivity:

> I am in your hands, do with me what you wish, the fear of death will not make me change my way of thinking. The King of Great Britain is my Prince. He nourished me, and I have sworn fidelity to him.[3]

Clark sent his second-in-command, Joseph Lawrence Bowman, who secured the rest of the Illinois villages without violence. Even Vincennes, across the Ohio River in modern Indiana, submitted peacefully. The town was later recaptured by the British and, after an epic march in winter, recovered by Clark.

3. Kathrine Wagner Seineke, *The George Rogers Clark Adventure in the Illinois* (Polyanthos, 1981), 262-64.

During the eighteenth century, victorious commanders frequently treated their defeated opponents with great generosity, treating them to lavish dinners and even allowing them parole so they might settle accounts locally and provide for their dependents. Clark's treatment of Rocheblave was markedly in contrast. Rocheblave was kept in close confinement, and he expressed distress and anxiety about his inability to provide for his wife, children, and the family of Hugh Lord whom he had been supporting.[4] Clark sent Rocheblave, bound in chains, into captivity at Williamsburg, where he was granted parole within the town, having given his word not to escape. When his captors transported him elsewhere, however, he felt free to make his escape, fleeing to New York, then held by the British. He remained in New York until 1781 when he was able to travel to Québec. After the end of the Revolutionary War, Rocheblave and his family made their home in Varennes, a suburb of Montreal. In the late 1780s and 1790s, Rocheblave became involved in the fur trade. The British authorities seem to have had little appreciation of his service in Illinois, and he found it difficult to recover back wages and losses he had suffered there. He sought trading licenses but again found no preferment that he regarded as due to him.

In 1796, Rocheblave was elected to the Legislative Assembly of Lower Canada. Feeling ignored and rejected by the British authorities, he allied himself with French Canadians. He was reelected in 1800 and served up to the time of his death in 1802. His sons, Pierre and Noël, were also elected to the Legislative Assembly.

Philippe-François de Rastel de Rocheblave was a man of the ancient régime, an aristocrat whose view of the world was hierarchical. Throughout his life he sought a king to whom he would be loyal and who would be loyal to him. In this he was disappointed by the French, Spanish, and British. A soldier and administrator rather than an explorer who opened new horizons, he was nevertheless important as a force who sought to establish order in the early Midwest.

4. Rocheblave to Guy Carleton, governor of the province of Québec and governor-general of British North America, citing *Canadian Archives*, Series B. 97, I: 1, translated in Mason, *Philippe de Rocheblave*, 289–90.

As a British administrator in Illinois, he has often been portrayed in a less than favorable light, but not all who opposed the Revolution ought to be regarded as villains.

CHAPTER EIGHT

TRADER AND PATRIOT

Daniel-Maurice Godefroy de Lincot

(1739–1783)

DANIEL-MAURICE GODEFROY DE LINCTOT was baptized on May 5, 1739, in Montreal (baptism usually followed quickly after birth). His family had for generations served in the French military, and Daniel-Maurice and his brothers Hyacinthe and Maurice-Régis all became officers. Their careers prior to 1760 cannot be easily distinguished. This much seems certain: By the early 1750s, Daniel-Maurice was a cadet, marked out for future promotion as an officer. He was the fifth generation Godefroy to serve in the military within New France, and in 1759 he became an ensign, the lowest rank of officer. After the English conquest of Canada, the family, like many others of the officer class, left the New France of Canada and North America and returned to France, but government support was not generous, particularly for officers who had served in the French marines in North America. In 1764, the three brothers, like many others from Canada, eventually came back to America. Daniel-Maurice became an Indian trader, operating out of Prairie du Chien in modern Wisconsin and Cahokia in Illinois.[1]

Daniel-Maurice Godefroy de Linctot was particularly known and respected for several reasons. His father, René Godefroy, Sieur de Linctot de Tonnancour, was a well-known and admired officer in the French marines, and Daniel-Maurice had also served with distinction during the French and Indian War. As a fur trader, Daniel-Maurice had earned a reputation for fair dealing and honesty. He had received as good an education as was available to a civilian, and he was renowned for his politeness and polished manners. He was also a linguist of ability and learned several Indian languages. The British repeatedly attempted to have Linctot enter British service, though he refused. After George Rogers Clark's capture of the Illinois Country, he became an enthusiastic supporter of the American cause. In 1779, Linctot, leading a force of Indians, defeated an expedition of Indians and British troops commanded by Charles Langlade and a Lieutenant Bennett sent from St. Joseph in order to attack Peoria. The British force was forced to retreat to St. Joseph.[2]

The French inhabitants of Illinois had never reconciled themselves to British rule, which was usually inept and often corrupt. Linctot may have also been influenced by the French inhabitants who were initially cordial and accepting of Clark's occupation with the cooperation of community leaders such as Father Pierre Gibault and Dr. Jean-Baptiste Laffont. The residents of Cahokia who were well ac-

1. For the general biography of Daniel-Maurice Godefroy de Linctot see Donald Chaput, "Godefroy de Linctot, Daniel-Maurice," *Dictionary of Canadian Biography*, http://www.biographi.ca/en/bio/godefroy_de_linctot_daniel_maurice_4E.htm; George A. Brennan, "De Linctot, Guardian of the Frontier," *Journal of the Illinois State Historical Society* 10, no. 3 (October 1917): 323–66. Some of Brennan's citations may be incorrect. F. L. Billon, *Annals of St Louis in its Early Days under the French and Spanish Dominations* (Printed for the Author, 1886; repr. Arno Press & *New York Times*, 1971); James Alton James, *George Rogers Clark papers 1771–1781* and *George Rogers Clark papers 1781–1784*, Collections of the Illinois Historical Library Volumes VIII–XIX; Virginia Series III–IV (Illinois State Historical Library, 1912–1926).

2. Peter Lawrence Scanlan, *Prairie du Chien: French, British, American* (George Banta Publishing Co., 1937), 67.

quainted with Linctot, elected him militia captain, in which capacity he eagerly cooperated with Clark. Linctot succeeded in convincing the Kaskaskia, Peoria, Piankeshaw, Wea, Kickapoo, and even some Sauk and Fox, to support Clark. The British were much alarmed by this activity, and Major Arent Schuyler DePeyster, the British commandant at Detroit, held the loyalty of the Miami and Potawatomi only by presenting great and expensive gifts, for which General Sir Frederick Haldimand, governor of Québec, criticized him. DePeyster assured Haldimand that without the presents and loyalty of the two tribes, the British presence in Detroit would be severely endangered.

Clark was so pleased with Linctot that he made him Indian agent of the Illinois department, from the Illinois to the Mississippi Rivers, while Captain Leonard Helm was placed in charge of the Wabash department, from the Illinois to Wabash Rivers. Clark also made Linctot major of the Virginian troops, an appointment subsequently approved by Thomas Jefferson, then governor of Virginia. Linctot went on an extensive scouting and recruiting expedition for Clark, to Peoria, Ouiateanon, and then returning to Vincennes. Although just a scouting expedition, it filled the British with alarm.

Hard currency, gold and silver coins, were exceptionally scarce in the Illinois Country, and Continental paper currency virtually worthless and seldom accepted. The fur trade, however, was active, and quality pelts were widely accepted at recognized values. Clark needed supplies, and Linctot lent pelts to Clark's quartermaster, Captain William Shannon, who issued the following certificates:

June 5, 1779.

On sight of this my exchange pleas pay order the sum of 3836 dollars and 2/5, it being received in your name and delivered to arrival at Fort Clark this 5 day of June, 1779.

William Shannon

June 5, 1779.

On sight please pay Mons. Capt. Langtot or order the sum of 7698 livres in cash for Peltrys furnished the State of Virginia for the use of purchasing provisions for said state.

Wm. Shannon.
Accepted G. R. Clark[3]

Linctot traveled to Virginia where he spent much of the winter of 1779–1780, and while there he conferred with the French admiral, Louis-Philippe de Rigaud de Vaudreuil, Marquis de Vaudreuil, who was particularly concerned to have Linctot ensure the support of the Illinois French for Clark. France had entered the war in support of the Revolution in 1778. By the summer of 1780, Linctot was at Fort Pitt, modern Pittsburgh, and from there he moved among the tribes of the Ohio valley, particularly the Delaware and Shawnee, encouraging them to support the American cause against the British. Linctot's mastery of several Indian languages undoubtedly proved an advantage in dealing with the tribes. The British commandant at Detroit, Arent Schuyler DePeyster, was so infuriated by Linctot's activity that he tried unsuccessfully to have the Indians take him and send him as a prisoner to Detroit. Linctot had several narrow escapes but continued to work for Clark.[4]

Clark repeatedly attempted to launch an attack on the British at Detroit, the center of supply for Indians who attacked Kentucky and threatened the Spanish in Upper Louisiana and the Americans in the Illinois Country. Clark made several attempts to organize expeditions against Detroit, but lack of resources ended them before they began. In 1780, Jefferson approved Clark's plans for yet another attempt to launch an expedition against Detroit. Linctot went to allied Indian tribes to rouse support for Clark's expedition, and Clark expected that Linctot would participate in the attack. Travel, hardships, and narrow escapes all effected Linctot's health, and he informed Clark that he was under a doctor's care but hoped to recover soon.[5]

3. Quoted in Brennan, "De Linctot," 328–29; also Clarence Walworth Alvord, ed. and intro, *Kaskaskia Records 1778–1790*, Collections of the Illinois State Historical Library, Volume V; Virginia Series Volume II (Illinois State Historical Library, 1909), 130–32.
4. Brennan, "De Linctot," 329–36.
5. C. W. Alvord, ed., *Cahokia records, 1778–1790* (Springfield, IL, 1907), Collections of the Illinois State Historical Library, Volume II; Virginia Series Volume I (Illinois State Historical Library, 1907), Linctot to Clark, July 31, 1781, 553–55.

It was not to be. Linctot seems to have died sometime between late 1781 and early 1783, only in his early forties.[6]

Clark's plan to attack Detroit, like those earlier, ended before it began. The Revolutionary War in the East was rapidly ending as French and American troops closed in on the British in the southern colonies. A subordinate of Clark's was badly defeated on the Ohio River, and Jefferson concluded that the expenditure of an expedition against Detroit was unnecessary.

Linctot's death was a tragedy for all the Midwest. His relations to the various Indian tribes and his earned reputation for honest dealings may have enabled him to avoid at least some of the conflicts between settlers entering the area and the tribes facing displacement.

6. Brennan, "De Linctot," 355, suggests Linctot died at St. Louis during the summer of 1781; James Alton James, *George Rogers Clark papers 1781–1784*, Collections of the Illinois Historical Library, Volumes XIX; Virginia Series IV (Illinois State Historical Library, 1926), 228–30; George Rogers Clark to the governor of Virginia (Benjamin Harrison), April 30, 1783, mentions that Linctot had died.

CHAPTER NINE

PROMISE UNFULFILLED

Joseph L. Bowman

(ca. 1752–1779)

JOSEPH LAWRENCE BOWMAN was born about 1752 in Frederick County, Virginia. He was of German descent, his surname was originally spelled "Baumann." His maternal grandfather, Jost Hite, settled in the Shenandoah Valley near modern Winchester, where Bowman was born. Bowman appears to have had a good education, especially for a youth in western Virginia, an area that was still somewhat wild. He could write correct English, although his understanding of French names sometimes produced strange spellings.[1]

1. Information about Joseph L. Bowman most often has to be gleaned from works mainly concerned with George Rogers Clark, such as William R. Nester, *George Rogers Clark: "I Glory in War"* (University of Oklahoma Press, 2012; Kenneth C. Carstens and Nancy Son Carstens, eds., *The Life of George Rogers Clark, 1752–1818* (Praeger, 2004); Lowell H. Harrison, *George Rogers Clark and the War in the West* (University Press of Kentucky, 1976; reprinted 2001); Milo Milton Quaife, ed., *The Conquest of the Illinois* (The Lakeside Press, 1920). There are many treatments of Clark. There are extensive bibliographies in Nester, *I Glory in War* and Stephen L. Kling Jr., Kristine L.

In 1774, Bowman took part in Lord Dunmore's War, during which he first became acquainted with George Rogers Clark and Leonard Helm, with both of whom he would serve in Illinois. After the war, Bowman moved to Kentucky where in 1776 at Harrodsburg he signed a petition seeking to establish Kentucky as a new county of Virginia. Early settlers in Kentucky frequently came into conflict with Indians who felt bitter about settler intrusion into land the Indians regarded as their own. In the autumn of 1777, thirty-seven men gathered at Bowman's property to shell corn when they were attacked by Indians. One settler was killed and six were wounded.

In early 1778 as George Rogers Clark was planning his invasion of British-controlled Illinois, he offered Bowman a commission if he could raise his own company. Bowman promptly raised a company and joined Clark's force in May. After traveling down the Ohio River, Clark's force landed in the vicinity of the old French fort at Massiac, later called Fort Massac, by modern Metropolis, Illinois. From there they traveled on foot across southern Illinois to Kaskaskia, the largest of the French villages in Illinois. Clark's approach went unnoticed, and his forces were able to secure the town without firing a shot.[2]

Clark's coup was well-received by the residents of Kaskaskia, particularly when it was announced that France had declared war on Britain in support of the Americans. Any replacement of British administration was also welcome. The British had long been traditional

Sjostrom, and Marysia T. Lopez, *The Battle of St. Louis, the Attack on Cahokia, and the American Revolution in the West* (THGC Publishing, 2017). A rare treatment of Bowman alone is in John W. Wayland, *The Bowmans: A Pioneering Family in Virginia, Kentucky, and the Northwest Territory* (McClure Co., 1943).

2. George Rogers Clark, *The Conquest of the Illinois*, Milo Milton Quaife, ed. (The Lakeside Press, 1920; reprint Southern Illinois University Press, 1992); George Rogers Clark, *Col. George Rogers Clark's Sketch of his Campaign in the Illinois in 1778–9; with an Introduction by Hon. Henry Pirtle, of Louisville, and an Appendix Containing the Public and Private Instructions to Col. Clark, and Major Bowman's Journal of the Taking of Post St. Vincents* (Ohio Valley Historical Series 3, 1869; reprint Applewood Books, 2008); George Rogers Clark's Memoir in James Alton James, *George Rogers Clark Papers 1771–1781*, Collections of the Illinois State Historical Library 8; Virginia Series 3 (Illinois State Historical Library, 1912), 220–24.

enemies, and their administration of the Illinois Country had been inept and sometimes corrupt.

At Clark's command, Bowman prepared for an expedition to the north to take the other French villages. He would be aided in this endeavor by the presence of several influential citizens of Kaskaskia who volunteered to accompany the expedition to expedite the peaceful transfer of control. About fifteen miles north of Kaskaskia, Bowman came to Prairie du Rocher, whose name he heard as "Parraderushi." He quickly took possession of the village and, encouraged by the presence of the French from Kaskaskia and the announcement of the French alliance, the citizens proved cooperative.

Nine miles north of Prairie du Rocher was the small village of St. Philippe. Bowman and his men arrived there in the middle of the night, initially scaring the inhabitants, who when day broke also showed themselves to be compliant. About forty-five miles north of St. Philippe, fronting on the Mississippi River, was the much larger town of Cahokia, whose name Bowman heard as "Cauhou." Again, Bowman arrived at night but was able to secure the town quickly. He took possession of a strong stone building, formerly the rectory of the Cahokia mission, which later served as a barracks for the British. Bowman was informed that a local citizen could raise 150 Indians to oppose the Americans, and Bowman quickly confined him under guard. In the morning, the citizens, again comforted by the French from Kaskaskia and the news of the French alliance, took an oath of loyalty.[3]

Bowman's men quickly converted the former rectory that served the British as a barracks into their own. The stone building was also a passable fortification, which was soon named "Fort Bowman." It would play an important role in the defense of Cahokia when the town, like St. Louis, was attacked by British-allied Indians led by a few pro-British French traders.

Clark recognized Bowman's success by having him promoted to the rank of major, and he was universally recognized as second-in-

3. Letter from Joseph Lawrence Bowman to Col. John Hite, in Wayland, *The Bowmans*, 74–76.

command to Clark. Bowman promptly involved himself in the civil administration of Cahokia, and he proved popular with the town's people. Shortly after the occupation, he introduced the first elected court of justice to Illinois, and the French elected Bowman as the first president of the court.

Early in the occupation of Illinois, Clark's forces had also secured Vincennes, located across the Wabash River in modern Indiana. There Captain Leonard Helm administered matters with only a small garrison. The British lieutenant governor Henry Hamilton, in command at Detroit, organized a large force composed of small contingents of English soldiers, French militia, and many Indians, and quickly retook Vincennes. The French militia and the Indians had to return to their homes to provide for their families during the winter. It would, in any case, have been impossible for Hamilton to provide for a large force at Vincennes for the entire winter. So, Hamilton dismissed all but a small garrison of British soldiers and a relatively few French, intending to reconstitute his force in the spring to attack Clark then. Hamilton disliked the people of Vincennes, who he regarded as uncouth and unreliable, and the local population detested Hamilton in turn.

Clark, aware of Hamilton's intensions, did not intend to remain passive until Hamilton attacked in the spring, but rather determined to attack Hamilton while most of the British force was absent. Clark's narrative description of the epic march to Vincennes, during which the troops had to wade through deep icy waters, is justly famous. Clark, however, waited to write his memoir ten or eleven years after the events in 1789 and 1790. By that time, Clark had fallen on difficulties, project after project had failed, and the memoir seemed to be an attempt to recapture some of the early glory. In the memoir, Clark is always the center and hero of the narrative. This is in great contrast to Bowman's description of events, always simple and modest, whether in the letter recounting events on the way to Cahokia or in his journal of the journey to Vincennes.[4]

4. The original manuscript of Bowman's journal, which is in poor condition, is with the Kentucky Historical Society. The section covering the advance to Vincennes was

A mural at the George Rogers Clark National Historical Park in Vincennes, Indiana, depicting the attack on Vincennes. The fort was less imposing than in the painting. (*National Park Service*)

Bowman and his troops played an important role in the siege of Vincennes, which surrendered to Clark after some resistance. The campaign to Vincennes was undoubtedly Clark's most impressive military achievement in Illinois and perhaps the high point in his life, but the celebration of the victory led to tragedy. Bowman, like other Kentuckians, was not averse to drinking, and during the celebration Bowman and others decided to fire a cannon. Muzzle loading artillery is inherently dangerous unless handled according to the

first published in *The Louisville Literary News*, a newspaper in Louisville, Kentucky, on November 24, 1840. The journal is most readily available in William Hayden English, *Conquest of the Country Northwest of the River Ohio 1778–1783 and Life of Gen. George Rogers Clark*, 2 vols. (The Bowen-Merrill Company, 1897) or James Alton James, *George Rogers Clark Papers 1771–1781*, Collections of the Illinois State Historical Library, vols. 8 and 19 (Illinois State Historical Library, 1912–1926).

strictest formal safety procedures, and alcohol is not conducive to the observation of such standards. While loading the cannon, several powder charges for the cannon exploded, badly burning Bowman and five others. Burns, especially large burns, are subject to infection, particularly on the frontier in the late eighteenth century where the germ theory was largely unknown and sanitation dubious at best. Bowman also seems to have suffered additional damage to his lungs and a significant concussion.

Bowman sought to overcome his severe burns, and in his memoire, Clark mentions Bowman as leading troops in June 1779, and in August he helped recruit men for Clark's planned campaign to Detroit, an expedition that never took place. Bowman, however, never fully recovered from the explosion, and on August 15, 1779, he died at Vincennes. He was buried there on August 18. He was only twenty-seven years old. Joseph Lawrence Bowman was a man of great ability, likeable, and admired by both Americans and French. He could have gone on to play a significant role in the development of the civil government after the end of the Revolution. His death was a loss for Illinois and all the Midwest.

CHAPTER TEN

FIRST ACROSS THE CONTINENT

Alexander Mackenzie

(1762–1820)

ALEXANDER MACKENZIE was born in 1762 at Stornoway on the Isle of Lewis in the Outer Hebrides of Scotland. The Scotland into which Mackenzie was born had changed greatly from the old Scotland of tradition in the wake of the unsuccessful Jacobite rebellions and the harsh English occupation of the country. Lairds now ignored the centuries-old loyalty to their chief men and the commoners who bore their clan names. They demanded rent for lands traditionally held for loyalty and service, but many people had little or no way of earning money. Crofters were driven from their homes, and sheep replaced families on the land. Mackenzie's family justly boasted a long and distinguished military history that had long been important in their clan, but now in the changed circumstances they found themselves losing social and economic status. They, like many thousands of other Scots, were driven to migration. Many

Scots served in foreign armies within the length and breadth of Europe, while others migrated to America.

After the death of his mother, Mackenzie, age twelve, sailed to New York with his father to join an uncle already in America.[1] When the American Revolution broke out, his father and uncle joined the King's Royal Regiment of New York, and in 1778, young Alexander was sent to Montreal. The city's population was a vibrant mixture of French, English, and Scots, whose businesses, especially the fur trade, were nurtured by two great rivers: the St. Lawrence River flowing from the northeast and the Ottawa River leading intriguingly to the west.

In 1779, young Mackenzie became an apprentice to Finlay, Gregory and Company, an important fur trading company. At first, he performed basic clerical duties such as filing papers and making copies of letters, but soon he was employed in more advanced tasks that allowed him to learn the fur trade accounting practices and details of shipping. When one of the partners, John Finlay, retired, Normand McLeod entered the firm, which in 1783 became Gregory, McLeod and Company. In 1784, Mackenzie went on his first trading mission, to Detroit. He did well there, and Gregory and McLeod

1. Alexander Mackenzie, *Voyages from Montreal, on the River St. Laurence. Through the Continent of North America, to the Frozen and Pacific Oceans; in the Years 1789 and 1793. With a Preliminary Account of the Rise, Progress and Present State of the Fur Trade of that Country* (Cadell & Davies, 1801) remains the basic source for Mackenzie. The work made him an international celebrity, and American, French, and German editions and even a Russian abridgement quickly followed the initial publication. Also of importance are W. Kaye Lamb, ed., *The Journals and Letters of Sir Alexander Mackenzie* (Cambridge University Press for the Hakluyt Society, Extra Series no. 41, 1970), which among many other important materials contains "General History of the Fur Trade" attributed to Roderick Mackenzie. Modern biographies include R. M. Ballantyne, *The Pioneers: A Tale of the Western Wilderness Illustrative of the Adventures and Discoveries of Sir Alexander Mackenzie* (James Nisbet, 1872); Mark S. Wade, *Mackenzie of Canada: The Life and Adventures of Alexander Mackenzie, Discoverer* (Blackwood, 1927); Walter Sheppe, ed. and commentary, *First Man West: Alexander Mackenzie's Journal of His Voyage to the Pacific Coast of Canada in 1793* (University of California Press, 1962); Roy Daniells, *Alexander Mackenzie and the North West* (Faber and Faber, 1969); Barry Gough, *First Across the Continent: Sir Alexander Mackenzie* (McClellan & Stewart, Inc., 1997).

extended the offer of a partnership to Mackenzie, provided he would go in the spring of 1785 to Grand Portage on the northwestern shore of Lake Superior to trade for the firm. Mackenzie quickly agreed and became a partner in the firm. Grand Portage was a center of the fur trade, where traders who lived among the Native peoples would come annually with the furs they had acquired for trade, rest, relaxation, celebration, and to some degree also dissipation. There, different partners were assigned various responsibilities, and Mackenzie took charge of the company's interests in a northern river of many names. The Natives called it the Missinipi and so it appears on Mackenzie's map. The river was also known as Churchill River after the name of the Hudson Bay Company fort at the river's mouth, founded in 1719. The waterway was additionally called the English River, and it appears under that name on maps today.

At about this same time, Mackenzie, like many others, took a Native "wife," nicknamed "The Catt," with whom he continued to associate when "up country" until her death in 1804.[2] In correspondence with his cousin Roderick Mackenzie, he refers to her as "Kitty." Undoubtedly, she helped him learn much about the Native people, knowledge that would be of great importance to him in the future. At this time Alexander also became a close friend of his cousin Roderick Mackenzie, nicknamed "Rory." Their correspondence reveals much about Alexander Mackenzie and the contemporary fur trade.[3] Mackenzie prospered greatly from trade around Lake Athabasca, and his careful and accurate geographic observations began to attract the attention of the wider world.

Mackenzie was a man of his age, and a major topic of interest at that time was the possibility of trade with China. The Russians had long been resident in Alaska and would continue to be until the czar's government sold the region to the United States in 1867. In the late eighteenth century, Russia, Great Britain, and even Spain, were in competition in northern waters above all for the fur of sea

2. Gough, *First Across*, 54, 178, 202–3.
3. Sheppe, *First Man*, 21–45, 51; Gough, *First Across*, 50–52, 74–76, 100–2.

otters that was in fashion and high demand in China. The ice-bound sea route to the north of Canada had proved impractical for trade, but the possibility of a land route through the Canadian wilderness still seemed a distinct possibility that appealed to Mackenzie. Many others were also interested in this possibility, such as Alexander Henry the Elder, Jonathan Carver, David Thompson, and the erratic, paranoid, and sometimes violent Peter Pond.

By 1786, Finlay, Gregory and Company established a post, Fort Chipewyan, on Lake Athabasca, and a small, advanced post on Great Slave Lake soon followed. Conflict between fur trade companies could be fierce and mutually destructive, and one way to limit the negative effects was to unite, and before the end of 1786 Finlay, Gregory and Company merged with the North West Company.

Mackenzie quickly realized that while Indigenous peoples well knew the geography of the immediate area in which they resided, their knowledge of distant areas was built on hearsay and could not be trusted. This was a lesson that some of his contemporaries never understood. Despite Mackenzie's skepticism concerning Native reports about distant geography, he was intrigued about rumors that a northern river led to a great body of salt water. If true, this could be the sought-after passage to the Pacific. It certainly seemed worth an investigation.

On June 3, 1789, Mackenzie, with a crew and several canoes, set out from Lake Athabasca heading first to Great Slave Lake[4] and from there to the river that the Native Dene people called and continue to call Deh-cho, literally "River Big." The name of the river on the official maps of Canada, however, is now the Mackenzie River. Mackenzie hoped that the river that flowed to the north would turn west and lead him to the Pacific Ocean.

In one canoe Mackenzie himself paddled along with a German, four Canadian men, three of whom were of French Canadian origin, and two of whom were accompanied by their wives. The second canoe was commanded by a Native called alternately English Chief

4. The name Great Slave Lake comes from the Cree Indians who raided the local Dene Tha' tribe of Athabaskan-speaking Indians for slaves.

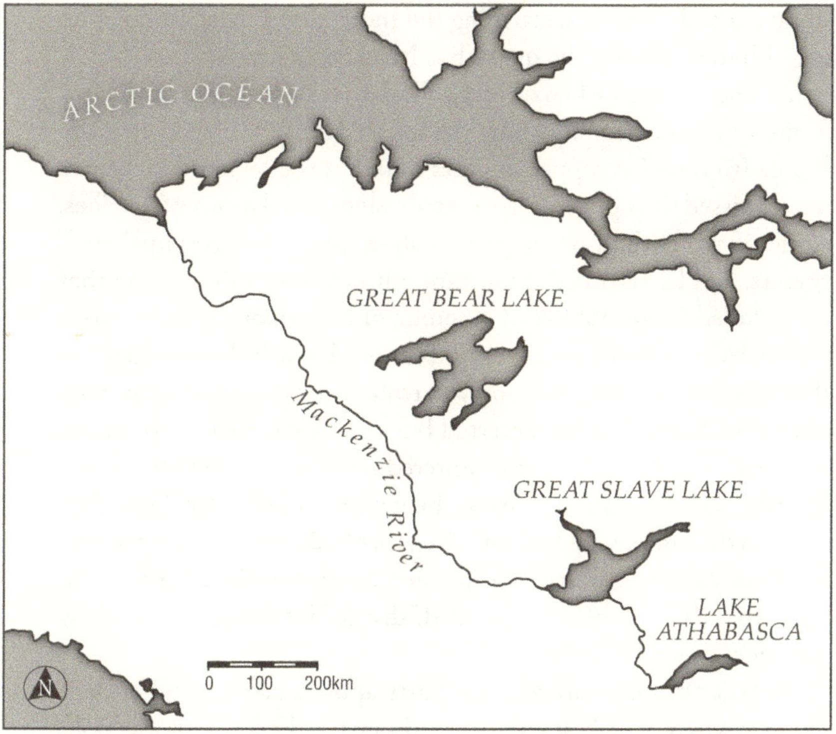

MacKenzie's route to the Arctic Ocean, 1789.

and Nestabeck by Mackenzie, accompanied by his two wives and two younger Native men. A third canoe also carried Natives who were to serve as hunters and interpreters. Yet another canoe, paddled by Indians, was under the command of Laurent Leroux, company clerk. It contained clothing, munitions, provisions, and trade goods. The Slave River leading to Great Slave Lake proved challenging, with many portages required by piles of driftwood and complicated by steep landing places and difficult currents. At Great Slave Lake, the men found it difficult to find the outlet to the river that Mackenzie wished to follow. Finally, on June 20 they came to the river and followed it ever northward. They encountered Native people who knew little about the farther extent of the river, but who told tales of rapids and monsters, alarming the Indians with Mackenzie, who urged him to give up the quest, but Mackenzie persisted.

At one point, Mackenzie met an Indian tribe he called the Yellow Knives, more commonly known as the Red Knives, since they made knives from native copper nuggets found in the region. Mackenzie never missed the opportunity to establish trade relations with tribes, some of which had never previously encountered Anglo-British traders, and he recorded important ethnographic information that he included in his published accounts of his explorations.[5] As they proceeded, the party came to rapids around which they portaged at the insistence of their guide, only to realize that the stream was quite navigable. Some Indians deserted but were lured back by presents. Mackenzie and company encountered more rapids, but the skilled French Canadian canoe men ran them without difficulty. Then they came to the ramparts where the river, that had been a mile-wide, was compressed into a narrow gorge only about hundred yards wide. After that the river became "braided," divided into many interlocking channels around islands.

A major problem arose as the party approached the end of their journey, where they first encountered signs of the local Inuit people. The Indians and Inuit had frequently been engaged in deadly hostilities, but fortunately the Inuit were not in the area, gone on their seasonal hunt for whales and caribou. Finally, Mackenzie concluded that what he had long suspected would be the case, that he had reached the Arctic Ocean rather than the Pacific. The quest for the Pacific would be reserved for another day.

The return, like all returns, was anticlimactic, but also wearying. The explorers continually had to fight rapid river currents, and they had to portage around rapids that they had been able to navigate while traveling downstream. Nevertheless, the men made remarkably good progress. Of course, they now knew where they were going and what to expect even though the Yellowknife guide soon deserted them. After 102 days travel and after having traversed over three

5. Mackenzie, *Voyages*. Mackenzie's ethnographic observations remain of importance to modern anthropologists.

thousand miles, Mackenzie and companions returned to Fort Chipewyan on Lake Athabasca. Mackenzie expressed disappointment that his exploration had not reached the Pacific, but he had opened much of the Canadian North to the fur trade and to further exploration and discovery, and Mackenzie's resolve to reach the Pacific remained strong.

MACKENZIE was above all a man of business, and it was not until 1792 that he was able to make another attempt to reach the Pacific Ocean. He departed late in the season on October 10, 1792, and obviously knew he could not reach the Pacific before the onset of winter. He would have to find a place to overwinter along the way. Mackenzie mentions only two canoes in connection with this expedition, loaded with trade goods, and with presumably about five or six paddlers for each canoe or a tota,l including Mackenzie, of only about a dozen men. Beginning at Fort Chipewyan, Mackenzie's crew proceeded a short distance up the Slave River and then turned west on the Peace River, so called because long before the Cree and Beaver Indians had met on the river to reach an accord to cease hostilities. So far, this was familiar territory to Mackenzie. Others had explored the Peace River and even established trading posts there.[6]

Near the confluence of the Peace and Smoky Rivers, Mackenzie established a substantial trading post, called Fort Fork, obviously intended to be a permanent installation. He sent men in advance who prepared the ground and materials for the new post. Mackenzie spent the winter trading for furs and planning the next stage in his campaign to reach the Pacific. When the weather warmed sufficiently in early May, Mackenzie had a canoe prepared twenty-five feet in length, sufficient to carry arms, ammunition, provisions, and presents for the Natives, all totaling about a ton and a half. The canoe carried ten men: five French Canadians, two Indians serving as hunters and interpreters, and three British Canadians, including Mackenzie himself.

6. Gough, *First Across*, 109–12.

The Peace River led Mackenzie into a land of mountains, rushing rivers, the Continental Divide, and a long, glaciated valley leading south by southeast. At the head of the valley, the Finlay River flowed into the long, narrow Williston Lake that essentially filled the valley, and from the southern end of the lake flowed the Parsnip River. The Peace River flowed from the southern portion of Williston Lake, and from there Mackenzie traveled on the Parsnip River south, looking always for a way west. The river proved difficult with frequent rocky rapids, some of which required laborious portages. Men grew discouraged, but Mackenzie persisted and encouraged his crew with ample lashings of rum. Along the Parsnip River, Mackenzie met the Sekani, a people who spoke an Athabaskan dialect. Initially reluctant to divulge information about the geography, they finally revealed that the Parsnip would take them to three small lakes between which they could portage, and that after the lakes they would encounter a creek that would lead them to a river that flowed to the west. For once the information was correct, but the creek proved dangerous. The crew lost control of a canoe that was essentially destroyed, with the loss of the lead balls for their guns, though they were able to save some gunpowder and shot. The crew, long experienced in the wilderness, built a new canoe, this time thirty feet long, the additional length to accommodate rolls of birchbark for repairs as they were heading into an area where birch trees were scarce. The creek, now known as James Creek, joined Herrick Creek. Herrick Creek soon flowed into the McGregor River. They followed the Fraser River until it met the Blackwater River that flowed west, finally bringing Mackenzie and his men to the village of Bella Coola, an inlet of the Pacific Ocean! There they encountered the Nuxalk, a Salish-speaking coastal people, who proved friendly and welcoming.

Mackenzie and his crew proceeded down the fjord-like inlet, visiting other villages and emerging into the coastal islands. Their reception by most of the Indigenous peoples was cordial, although one group had previously had a bad experience with Europeans and were only reconciled with difficulty. On a convenient rockface, Mackenzie painted the following inscription in a mixture of vermilion and melted grease:

Alex Mackenzie
From Canada
by land
22d July 1793

That concoction would not preserve the writing for long, but subsequent travelers engraved the message on the rock, where it remains visible today.

The return, like that from the Arctic Ocean, went relatively quick as they now knew where they were going. Mackenzie suffered from swollen ankles from cold water when the canoe had to be portaged and at one point had to be carried, but by August 24 they had returned to Fort Fork. The grand adventure was concluded, and with it the end of Mackenzie's explorations. Mackenzie had, however, opened an entirely new area to the fur trade, and members of the North West Company were not slow to exploit it. Scarcely had Mackenzie returned before others penetrated the area, found even faster and easier ways to reach the Pacific and the profitable trade with China, although the trek long remained economically impractical.

Henceforth, Mackenzie would be devoted to business. After a long and boring winter at Athabasca, Mackenzie traveled to Grand Portage for the annual meeting of the "wintering partners" of the North West Company. Mackenzie's achievement was recognized by the grant of an additional share in the company. The partners of the company were divided into two groups: the Canadian "wintering partners" who traded for the furs that supported the company and the shareholders in England who sold the furs. The Canadian partners felt that the London business managers paid too little attention to the Canadian's problems and needs, and expected that Mackenzie, with his new-found prominence, would represent them to the London managers. He did so, but the struggle to gain more representation for the Canadian partners took until 1804.

In 1794, Mackenzie made the acquaintance of Major John Graves Simcoe, the lieutenant governor of Upper Canada. Mackenzie promoted the idea of the North West Company transferring furs to posts on the Pacific coast, particularly to promote trade with China, rather than hauling them all the way to the Atlantic coast, shipping them to London, and then via India to China. Simcoe thought the plan practical and advantageous and reported so to the Committee of the Privy Council for Trade and Foreign Plantations to the House of Lords. Governor Dorchester in Montreal was also enthusiastic about the plan, and Mackenzie was soon on the way to London to promote the scheme further.

Dissent arose within the North West Company. Many furs sent to London were consumed in the local market, and shipping furs directly to China weakened the London market, particularly in competition with the Hudson's Bay Company that was the chief competitor of the North West Company. Members of the company in Montreal were also disturbed by the loss of trade coming through that center. Nevertheless, Mackenzie was convinced that the future of fur trade was tied to the Pacific Northwest and the trade with China. The Chinese paid high premiums for choice furs, especially the luxurious fur of the sea otter. In Europe, Chinese goods, both tea and porcelains, were then greatly in fashion and those of the best quality brought high prices.

Mackenzie had little tolerance for those who did not agree with his view of the future fur trade. A frequent object of his hostility was a fellow Scot, Simon McTavish, an important figure in the North West Company. Mackenzie and McTavish had been in conflict as early as Mackenzie's exploration to the Arctic in 1789. McTavish made no mention of Mackenzie's achievement in opening new territory to the fur trade but criticized him for failure to attend to business and sending only a small number of inferior furs to Montreal. McTavish promoted his nephew William McGillivray, despite inexperience, rather than Mackenzie, who felt grossly insulted. McTavish also opposed Mackenzie's vision of fur trade centered in the Pacific Northwest, arguing that Montreal ought to remain the fur trade center. Most of the "wintering' partners supported Mackenzie, but McTavish controlled enough votes of those centered in Montreal and London to defeat Mackenzie's initiatives. Mackenzie increasingly vented his frustrations in frequent angry and petulant behavior.

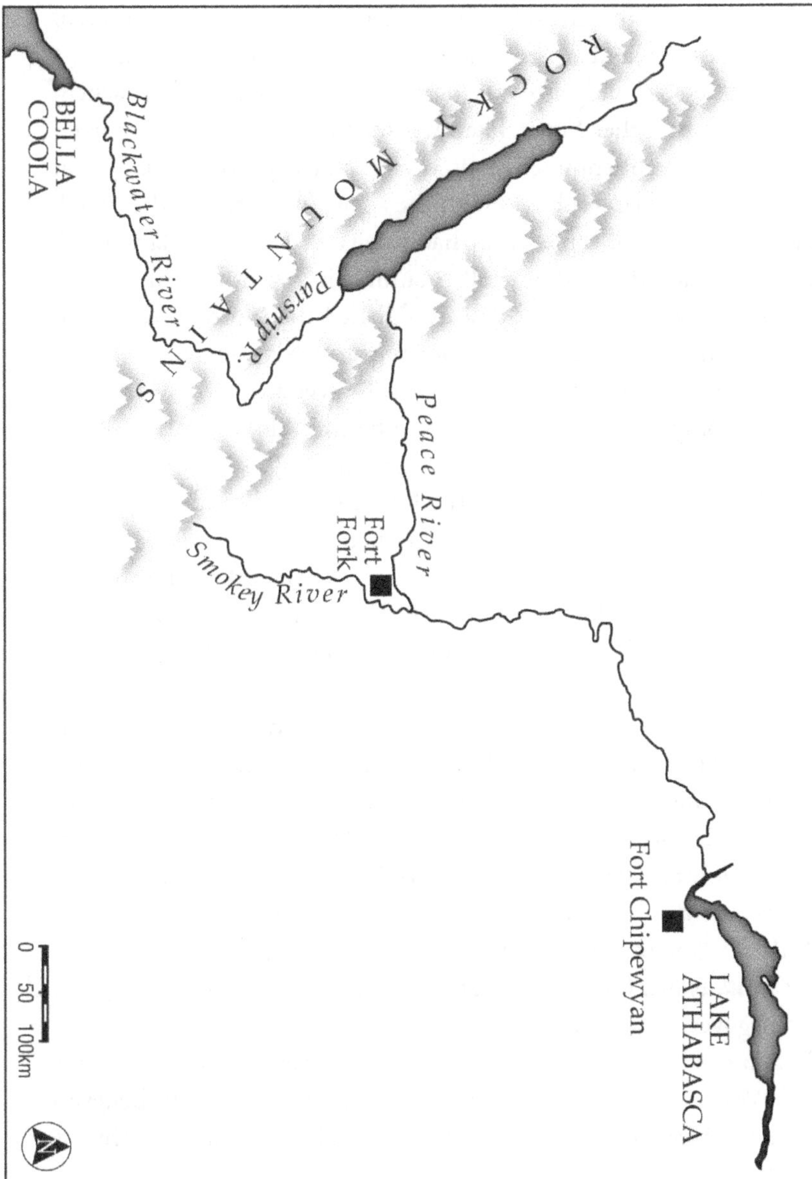

Mackenzie's route to the Pacific Ocean.

The late eighteenth and early nineteenth centuries were times of heavy drinking, and a man who could not hold his liquor during a long evening of indulgence was hardly counted a man at all. Mackenzie, like many other Scots, liked whiskey, and the fur trade parties in Montreal frequently terminated with all the partners passed out on the floor. This, combined with the rigors of winters in the North and exhaustions of exploration, had a negative effect on Mackenzie's health, though that did not fully manifest itself until late in his life.

In 1799, the agreement that established the North West Company expired and it reformed, but without Mackenzie. After the partners met at Grand Portage, the last he ever attended, Mackenzie left the company. He may have had a hand in the formation of the New North West Company, nicknamed the XY Company. The North West Company had marked their bales of goods "NW," and the new company marked theirs "XY," hence the moniker. The New North West Company was smaller than its namesake, but more aggressive, and soon found itself in rivalry with the old North West Company, the Hudson's Bay Company, and the equally aggressive John Jacob Astor.

In 1800 and 1801, Mackenzie repeatedly traveled between London and Montreal. Despite Mackenzie's breach with the North West Company, his association with it had made him wealthy, and in London he associated with the social elite. In 1801, he published *Voyages from Montreal, on the River St. Laurence. Through the Continent of North America, to the Frozen and Pacific Oceans; in the Years 1789 and 1793. With a Preliminary Account of the Rise, Progress and Present State of the Fur Trade of that Country*, and later that year he presented a proposal to the government, entitled "Preliminaries to the Establishment of a Permanent British Fishery and Trade in Furs etc. on the Continent and West Coast of North America," fully outlining what he believed to be the best plans for the development of the Pacific Northwest coast.

Walter Sheppe points out that Alexander Mackenzie had only a few years of formal education, yet the accounts of his expeditions to the Arctic and Pacific are written in a correct and literate style. Most texts by explorers with similar education are semiliterate. It seems

Portrait of Alexander Mackenzie by Thomas Lawrence, 1800. (*National Gallery of Canada*)

certain that Mackenzie hired a writer who would remain anonymous to turn his journals and notes into good prose. Mackenzie apparently employed William Combe, who specialized in preparing travelers' journals for publication. Combe made a list of the works he edited, and Mackenzie's *Voyages* appears on that list. The employment of such editors was common and accepted. Mackenzie's original papers were lost in 1832 when his estate, Avoch, burned.[7]

Voyages, dedicated to King George III, was an instant success and attracted the attention of Edward, Duke of Kent, son of King George III and father of future Queen Victoria. The duke was largely responsible for Mackenzie receiving a knighthood in 1802.[8] Mackenzie's old comrades in Canada reacted to his newfound dignity with a mixture of respect and satire, never missing an opportunity to refer to him formally as Sir Alexander Mackenzie.

Mackenzie now traveled repeatedly between Montreal and London, seeking to promote his Pacific coast vision. In 1802, he formally joined the New North West Company, and in 1804 he was elected

7. Sheppe, *First Man*, "Appendix Three: Note on the Text," 337–39.

8. The work made Mackenzie an international celebrity. For the involvement of Edward, Duke of Kent, see Gough, *First Across*, 178.

to the Quebec legislature, but he soon found politics not to his liking and resigned. McTavish, Mackenzie's great rival, died in 1804, setting the stage for the eventual merger of the New North West Company and the older North West Company.

Mackenzie had grown wealthy, but the rigors of his explorations, winters in northern Canada, and colossal drinking bouts were taking a toll, prematurely aging him. In 1805, he left Canada for the last time, retiring to Scotland, where he purchased an estate and married a woman who became Lady Geddes Mackenzie. They had three children, born between 1816 and 1819. Mackenzie assumed the role of benevolent squire in the area surrounding his estate, traveled occasionally with Edward, Duke of Kent, and he and his wife enjoyed a town house in London, which they visited for part of the year. Mackenzie's health worsened, and in 1820 while traveling in Scotland, he collapsed and died. His death has been attributed to Bright's disease, an affliction of the kidneys, perhaps aggravated by cirrhosis of the liver. He was fifty-six years old.

CHAPTER ELEVEN

FRONTIER VENGEANCE

Lewis Wetzel

(ca. 1763–1808)

Tom Quick

(1734–1796)

LEWIS WETZEL was born about 1763 either in Lancaster County, Pennsylvania, or in what is now West Virginia on the South Branch of the Potomac River. His father, John Wetzel, was German or Swiss and had come to America as an indentured servant. His mother was of Flemish heritage. By 1770, the family was certainly living in what is now northern West Virginia about fourteen miles from Fort Henry. Lewis had four brothers and two sisters who survived into adulthood.[1]

1. Lewis Wetzel has been the subject of several biographies, mainly written in the nineteenth century. They universally ignore and suppress the dark aspects of his personality

In 1774, Iroquois chief Logan's family was murdered by Virginians at the Yellow Creek Massacre. This act led to retaliatory Indian raids that helped provoke Lord Dunmore's War that same year. Raids continued after the conclusion of that brief military confrontation. When Lewis was about fourteen years old, he and his brother were kidnapped by Indians. Lewis was also grazed across the chest by a bullet, leaving an injury that was painful although not serious. The Indians failed to secure their captives at night, and the boys were able to escape and return home. In 1786, Wetzel's father, a brother, and a sister were all killed by Indians during a raid, which seemed to have engendered a fierce hatred of all Indians in him. He made no distinction between friendly and unfriendly Indians, eagerly slaughtering any Indian he could.

Judge Foster described Wetzel in 1789 when he was about twenty-six years old as about five feet ten inches tall, broad shouldered, and heavily muscled. He had a relatively dark complexion heavily pitted from smallpox. His eyes were black and described as piercing. He was proud of his hair, which he seems to have considered, like Samson in the Bible, as the source of his strength. It eventually reached the calves of his legs. He clubbed his hair, plaiting it, and securing it with ribbons in a style favored by frontiersmen in

and treat him as a hero. See Cecil B. Hartley, *Life and adventures of Lewis Wetzel, the Virginia rancher; to which are added biographical sketches of General Simon Kenton, General Benjamin Logan, Captain Samuel Brady, Governor Isaac Shelby, and other heroes of the West* (G. G. Evans, 1859); Charles McKnight, *Our Western Border* (J. C. McCurdy & Co., 1876); Edward Sylvester Ellis, *The life and times of Col. Daniel Boone, hunter, soldier, and pioneer: with sketches of Simon Kenton, Lewis Wetzel, and other leaders in the settlement of the West* (Porter & Coates, 1884); Robert Cornelius V. Meyers, *Life and adventures of Lewis Wetzel, the renowned Virginia ranger and scout, comprising a thrilling history of this celebrated Indian fighter with his perilous adventures and hair-breadth escapes, and including other interesting incidents of border life* (International Book Company, 1883). More recently but in the same vein, Clarence Brent Allman, *Lewis Wetzel, Indian fighter; the life and times of a frontier hero* (Devin-Adair Co., 1961). The author is Wetzel's great-nephew. A notable correction is Brian D. Hardison and Ray Swick, "A Recruit for Aaron Burr: Lewis Wetzel and the Burr 'Conspiracy,'" *West Virginia History* 3, no. 2 (2009): 75–86. The most valuable source for Lewis Wetzel is Samuel Brady & Lewis Wetzel papers, OCLC: (OCoLC)ocm03854181; The Draper manuscript collection. Series E: v. 1–16.

the late eighteenth century. Wetzel's earlobes were slit, and he wore long silk tassels in them.[2]

Wetzel was famous for his ability to load his gun while at a full run. He was aided in doing this by keeping several slightly undersized lead balls in this mouth that he could quickly spit down the barrel of his gun. As a result, late in life Wetzel may have shown symptoms of lead poisoning. In a famous escapade he was pursued by four Indians, but loading as he ran, he managed to kill three of them; the fourth broke off the pursuit.[3] In close combat Wetzel favored the tomahawk, although he was reputedly skilled with a knife as well. In one instance, he crept into an Indian's camp and used his knife to slay the man as he slept.

There are many tales of Wetzel's attacks on Indians, but few were documented. It does seem apparent that Wetzel lost no opportunity to kill Indians, whether friendly or not, often from ambush. The Draper manuscripts contain accounts, but many of them were not recorded until years after the events, and some told by people not involved in the matter. Such accounts are naturally subject to exaggeration. Wetzel supposedly never attacked women or children, but upon occasion he exhibited extreme brutality.

In 1785, General Josiah Harmar, who was later disastrously defeated by the tribes on the Upper Wabash, built Fort Harmar near the confluence of the Muskingum and Ohio Rivers, modern Marietta, Ohio, and there in 1789 he called a peace conference between the United States and representatives of the much-weakened Ottawa, Wyandot, Chippewa, Potawatomi, Sauk, Iroquois, and Lenape (Delaware) tribes. Wetzel almost ruined the conference before it began. He and a companion named Veach Dickerson ambushed a prominent and peaceful Indian who was riding to the meeting, shooting him in the back. The Indian, severely wounded, reached the fort but soon died. Harmar ordered the arrest of Wetzel, who was taken but managed to escape. He was recaptured, but poorly guarded, perhaps on purpose, and he again escaped. Settlers pre-

2. McKnight, *Our Western Border*, 339.
3. Ibid., 336–39.

vented Harmar's troops from retaking Wetzel, and he was never punished for the murder.

One notable instance of Wetzel's cruelty took place at Fort Massac, at modern Metropolis, Illinois, then occupied by US troops. Visiting there, Wetzel found a drunk Indian sleeping face down. Stealing a soldier's ramrod, he loaded it into his gun and shot it up the Indian's posterior, killing him. The officers examined the soldiers until they found one missing his ramrod. The soldier was condemned for the killing despite his insistence that he was innocent. Just as he was about to be executed, Wetzel came forward and claimed the crime. He then fled before he could be caught.[4] One instance where Wetzel was not able to avoid prosecution occurred when he visited New Orleans. While there he became involved in a counterfeiting scheme. In this instance he was apprehended, convicted, and imprisoned for nearly two years. Some remarked that he seemed much changed after his imprisonment, but they do not explain in what way.

After Aaron Burr killed Alexander Hamilton in a duel, his political life in Washington was at an end. Burr searched for a project that would restore his reputation, which led to a great conspiracy involving Spanish Texas. Nancy Isenberg argues that in 1807 Burr hoped to conquer Spanish Texas and add it to the United States rather than, as often supposed, to establish an independent country.[5] Nevertheless, the attempt was ill-considered, reckless, and could easily have involved the United States in a war with Spain just at the time when the United States' relationship with Great Britain was deteriorating. Recent evidence indicates that Wetzel joined Burr's forces, another indication of Wetzel's chaotic character.[6]

A relative of Wetzel, Philip Sikes, lived about twenty miles from Natchez in the interior, and there Wetzel settled in the early nine-

4. Draper Manuscripts 9 S174; recounted in Brian D. Hardison and Ray Swick, "A Recruit for Aaron Burr," *West Virginia History* 3 no. 2 (2009): 79. Fort Massac was occupied by US troops from 1794 to 1814.

5. Nancy Isenberg, *Fallen Founder: The Life of Aaron Burr* (Penguin Books, 2008), 319–65.

6. Brian D. Hardison and Ray Swick, "A Recruit for Aaron Burr," 79.

teenth century, and there he died in the summer of 1808. There is no firm evidence about the cause of his death, although some accounts indicate a fever of unspecified type led to his end. He was about forty-four or forty-five years old.

It is generally not useful to attribute modern mental analysis to historical figures who lived in a world much different than our own. Wetzel's failure, however, to distinguish between friendly and unfriendly Indians, lack of compassion, and his brutal behavior may indicate an unwillingness to forgive the murders of family members, which may have led to mental instability. His brutality and murder of even friendly Indians brought him to the attention of the law, but he repeatedly managed to escape prosecution. In a world where confrontations between Indians and intrusive settlers were common, settlers tended to regard him as a hero and aided him in avoiding the law. His imprisonment in New Orleans on the charge of counterfeiting seems anomalous, but it may indicate a lawless orientation, as does his alliance with Aaron Burr.

THE LIFE OF TOM QUICK provides a strange parallel to that of Lewis Wetzel. Quick was born in 1734 in Milford, Pennsylvania. He was the youngest or next to the youngest among ten children born to Thomas Quick and Margriete Decker, also spelled Dekker. So much seems to be fact, but much of Quick's biography is mired in popular and largely fictional accounts.[7]

7. Like Wetzel, "histories" of Tom Quick were written primarily in the nineteenth century, and they also tend to suppress the murderous aspect of Quick's behavior and treat him as a hero. See James Eldridge Quinlan, *Tom Quick, the Indian Slayer, and the Pioneers of Minisink and Wawarsink* (De Voe & Quinlan, 1851); William Bross, *Legend of the Delaware:* An *Historical Sketch of Tom Quick; to which is Added the Winfield Family: also, Miscellaneous Papers and Articles* (Knight and Leonard, Chicago, 1887); Abraham Sylvester Gardiner, *Tom Quick, or, The Era of Frontier Settlement: Notes and Supplementary Facts suggested by the "Legend of the Delaware"* (Knight & Leonard Co., Printers, 1888); Abraham Sylvester Gardiner, *Tom Quick, or The Foundation and the Capstone. Pioneer Enterprise and National Independence* (Knight & Leonard Co., 1889); James Eldridge Quinlan, *The Original Life and Adventures of Tom Quick, the Indian Slayer* (Deposit Journal, 1894).

According to tradition, Quick grew up familiar with the Lenape (Delaware) Indians and became fluent in their language. Both the French and British sought to use the Lenape for their own purposes during the French and Indian War. The French were most successful in recruiting the Lenape, which led to conflicts with the English-speaking settlers. According to tradition, during the winter Quick, his father, and another relative were cutting hoop poles, usually sapling wood of hickory or white oak, used for barrel hoops before the use of strap iron became common. They were ambushed by the Lenape, and Quick's father was badly wounded. Realizing his wound was mortal, he urged the others to abandon him and run for their lives. Looking back, Quick saw the Indians kill and scalp his father.

After the Indians departed, Quick and other members of the family gave Thomas Sr. a decent burial, after which Tom Quick supposedly swore a fearful oath. Taking his knife in his right hand and holding a bullet in his left, he reportedly swore:

> By the point of the knife in my right hand and the deadly bullet in my left; by heaven and all that there is in it; by earth and all that there is on it; by the love I bore my father, there on his grave I swear eternal vengeance against the whole Indian race. I swear to kill all and spare none; the old man with his silver hair, the lisping babe without teeth; the mother quick with child and the maiden in the bloom of youth shall die.[8]

The oath is highly rhetorical, even theatrical, more than one would expect from a backwoods man of limited education. The entire oath may be no more than a scene from a now lost vaudeville production about Quick's life. So it is with many of the traditions associated with Tom Quick. Supposedly, he hunted Indians much like Lewis Wetzel, and like Wetzel, his murders appear to be brutal. Reportedly, Quick continued to kill long after the end of the French and Indian War and official establishment of peace.

8. James M. Allerton, *Hawk's Nest, or The Last of the Cahoonshees: A Tale of the Delaware Valley and Historical Romance of 1690* (Port Jervis, NY: The Gazette Book & Job Print, 1892), 222. This quotation is likely little more than a product of oral tradition.

In his later years, he became talkative and related stories about hunting and killing Indians. Quick's claims were primarily recounted by Quick himself. He said he killed about one hundred Indians, though others claim he was responsible for a much smaller number, perhaps about twenty. Still, his stories depict simple murders, and like Wetzel's reported slaughters, most cannot be verified. Quick, like Wetzel, lived in a period when story telling was a chief form of amusement, and there was little care whether the tales were true or not. Even newspapers printed obviously false stories, often assuming that the readers would not take them seriously.[9] Lack of specific context protected Quick from prosecution, but eventually even settlers began to feel that his claimed behavior was excessive.

Quick eventually retired to live at the home of Jacobus Rosencranz, also spelled Rosencrance, at or near Matamoras, Pennsylvania, and there he died supposedly from smallpox in 1796. According to legend, Indians dug up his body and distributed portions to various groups that had suffered at his hands, but the remains spread smallpox among the Indians. Like most stories associated with Tom Quick, it is highly dubious.

In 1889, William Bross, a descendant of Tom's brother Jacobus and author of an early flattering biography of Tom Quick, erected

9. Arthur K. Moore, "Specimens of the Folktales from Some Antebellum Newspapers of Louisiana," *Louisiana Historical Quarterly* 32, no. 4 (October 1949), 723–58. The pioneer folklorist Arthur K. Moore describes these practices as owing in large measure to the catholicity of taste possessed by many a whimsical editor and to lack of adequate sources of conventional news. Editors permitted themselves wide latitude in supplying a mélange of imitative verse by hometown muses, sketches of local characters, reports of traditional observances, superstitions, and prejudices and fabulous narratives. Newspapers were replete with tales of the discovery of hidden treasures and usually subsequent loss, hidden mines, mysterious inscriptions, strange creatures glimpsed in the forest, gigantic skeletons, and similar wonders. Journalists, orators, and politicians routinely created mythic stories to entertain their audiences. Moore focused primarily on Louisiana newspapers, but the same tendency prevailed in newspapers elsewhere. Examples can be cited in great number, but one of the most obvious is the account of an underground city supposedly discovered by coal miners 360 feet below Moberly, Missouri. The story is still taken seriously by denizens of the internet, who apparently fail to realize the story originated in the local newspaper that published the tale, suggestively, on April 1, 1885.

An early twentieth-century postcard of the monument to Tom Quick "Indian Slayer" in Milford, Pennsylvania.

the Settlers Monument, more generally called the Tom Quick Monument in Milford. Quick's remains were disinterred from his burial place at Matamoras and transferred to Milford, something hardly possible if Indians had previously dug up the body. Someone shattered the monument in 1997, and while it was rebuilt, it was not returned in place because Native Americans and others protested the restoration.

CHAPTER TWELVE

PIONEER OF KENTUCKY

Simon Kenton

(1755–1836)

SIMON KETON was born in Prince William County in northeastern Virginia on April 3, 1755.[1] His father was an immigrant from Ireland and his mother of mixed Scot and Welsh heritage. They were tenant farmers. Simon was the seventh born of nine children. He had three older brothers and three older sisters,

1. Robert E. Coleman,"Simon Kenton," *Harper's New Monthly Magazine*, 28 (165) (February 1864), 289–304; Cecil B. Hartley, *Life and Adventures of Lewis Wetzel, The Virginia Ranger: To Which are Added Biographical of General Simon Kendon, General Benjamin Logan ... and Other Heroes of the West* (Hurst & Co., 1904); Edna Kenton, *Simon Kenton: His Life and Period, 1755–1836* (Doubleday, Doran & Co., 1930); Thomas Dionysius Clark, *Simon Kenton: Kentucky Scout* (originally published 1943; repr., Jesse Stuart Foundation, 1993); Patricia Jahns, *The Violent Years: Simon Kenton and the Ohio-Kentucky Frontier* (Hastings House, 1962); Allen W. Eckert, *The Frontiersmen* (Little, Brown & Company, Inc., 7th printing, 1980); Karen Meyer, *Simon Kenton Unlikely Hero: Biography of a Frontiersman* (Sable Creek Press, 2018).

and one younger brother and one younger sister. The other children of the family seem to have achieved basic literacy, but Simon remained illiterate throughout his life. He eventually learned to sign his name mechanically, laboriously copying an example provided for him. He grew to be a large man, about five feet ten inches in height, thus taller than most of his contemporaries. His face was dominated by a large nose and jaw.

Little is known of Kenton's early life, but in 1771 at the age of sixteen he got in a fight with William Leachman, the name is also written Leitchman, over the affections of a girl. Believing that he had killed Leachman, Kenton fled to western Virginia, where he assumed the name "Simon Butler." Eventually discovering that Leachman had recovered and married the young woman, Simon would later return to his real name.

Fascinated by accounts of far western Virginia and Kentucky, Kenton partnered with two other young men, named Yager and Strader. The three trapped and hunted successfully for some time in what is now West Virginia, Kenton and Strader doing most of the hunting while Yager prepared the skins. In March of 1773, their camp was raided by Indians. Yager was killed immediately, and the other two fled without even their shoes or rifles. After five days without food, they stumbled into a family who had built a cabin in the wilderness. The family generously fed and clothed them, and, after leaving the kind family, the pair encountered a party on the Kanawa River headed toward Kentucky, which they joined. All did not go well, however. Encountering a hostile war party, the group abandoned their boats and retreated to Virginia. Kenton, just eighteen years old at the time, acted as a guide as they moved through the wilderness. This feat added greatly to his reputation.

In 1774, the Shawnee, Delaware (Lenape), and Wyandot, outraged by the violence of settlers against Indians, rose and attacked settlers along the frontier. Many families abandoned their holdings and retreated to safer areas in Virginia. John Murray, Lord Dunmore, raised forces to oppose the Indians in what became known as Lord Dunmore's War. Kenton became a scout for Dunmore's troops. In this capacity he became acquainted with and developed a friendship with Simon Girty, a man whose subsequent reputation during the Revolution struck terror in settlers. Along with his two brothers, the three Girtys worked for the British, and had a reputation for extreme brutality. George Rogers Clark also took part in Lord Dunmore's War, but there is no documented evidence that he met Kenton at this time.

Another acquaintance, Jake Drennon, assisted Kenton in an attempt to raise a company of men for Lord Dunmore's War, but they were unable to enroll an entire company, so the men raised were incorporated into George Rogers Clark's company. Kenton and Drennon acted as "spies," that is, scouts for the company. The first campaign in which Kenton played a role was against the Muskingum Indians, a group of the Delaware (Lenape) people. Kenton and Drennon enabled the troops to avoid an ambush, and the troops destroyed several Indian towns and burned their crops. The war ended when troops under the command of Andrew Lewis won the Battle of Point Pleasant in October of 1774. In the Treaty of Camp Charlotte, the Indians agreed to the Ohio River as the demarcation line between Indian lands and the lands on which settlers were permitted.

After the war, Kenton partnered with Thomas Williams, and the pair explored and even raised a modest corn crop in Kentucky. In 1775, there was peace on the frontier and Kenton, still going under the name Simon Butler, visited all the new settlements and became familiar with all the trails and even war paths throughout Kentucky. He served as guide and advisor to many new settlers entering Kentucky.

In 1776, matters changed radically. The Revolutionary War was underway, and the British supplied the Indians and encouraged them to attack American settlers. Warfare broke out across Kentucky, and many of the settlers who had arrived the previous year abandoned their holdings and retreated into Virginia. Kenton, still using the name Butler, was at Harrodsburg when John Gabriel Jones and George Rogers Clark were selected to represent Kentucky to the Virginian legislature and executives seeking aid against the Indians. Kenton may have first met Clark on this occasion.

The year 1776 was difficult for settlers, but 1777 was even worse. Most settlements that had begun with great hopes and expectations were abandoned in the face of Indian raids, except for Boonesborough, Harrodsburg, and Logan's Station, also known as St. Asaph. Those who had not fled to Virginia congregated at these three locations. Logan's Station, the weakest of the three, was subject to a thirteen-day siege led by the Chillicothe Shawnee war chief Blackfish that year.

The Virginia government commissioned George Rogers Clark as military commander of Kentucky early in 1777. Although Clark was not provided with any money for scouts, he appointed five, including Simon Kenton. Clark's force was insufficient to eliminate Indian raids, but it was important that the Virginia government, despite the continuing Revolution against Britain in the East, nevertheless acknowledged the importance of protecting the settlers in Kentucky.

Blackfish and his men attacked Boonesborough in late April. Kenton and a couple of other men pursued a small group of Indians who attacked two men who had just left the fort, and Daniel Boone with ten more men came to support Kenton. A large group of Indians attempted to surround Boone and the others, but Boone ordered his men to retreat to the fort. Kenton shot one Indian who was aiming at Boone, but that did not spare Boone. He was wounded in the leg, breaking the bone. Kenton killed another Shawnee as the Indian was about to tomahawk Boone, and then relying on his unusual size and strength, Kenton picked up Boone and ran an evasive course so the Indians could not fire upon them accurately. Bearing Boone, Kenton reached the gate of the fort, followed closely by others who had been wounded and those who had not. They were able to close the gate and keep the Indians out. Blackfish maintained the siege for several days and then withdrew. Saving Boone contributed greatly to Kenton's reputation. Boone recovered from both the wound and the broken leg, but he required significant time to recuperate.

In 1778, Kenton raided into Indian territory across the Ohio River to recover stolen horses. The first attempt succeeded, but a second attempt on the large Shawnee town of Chillicothe (now Old-

A 1784 map of Kentucky. Harrodsburg is to the left and across the river from the letter "L" in Lincoln at lower right; Logan's Station is below the "L"; while Boonesborough is above and across the river from the letter "N" in Lincoln. (*Library of Congress*)

town, Ohio) miscarried and Kenton was taken prisoner. He was forced to run a quarter-mile gauntlet between lines of Indians who struck him with sticks and clubs. The Shawnee admired Kenton's endurance and made him repeatedly run the gauntlet, a total of six times. The sixth time, he broke through the line of tormentors and escaped briefly but was recaptured. The Shawnee intended to burn Kenton at the stake, but at the last moment Simon Girty, then working for the British, arrived in the Indian camp and at least temporarily saved Kenton from the stake. The Shawnee soon concluded that Kenton was too great an enemy to be allowed to live and decided to execute him at the British trading post at Upper Sandusky. The Indians broke Kenton's arm and collarbone on the way to the execution. The Shawnee chief Logan, who sought peace with the settlers, pled for Kenton's life, and Captain Pierre Drouillard,[2] Logan's envoy, impressively dressed in full uniform and regalia arrived just as Kenton was about to be burned. Drouillard presented gifts and convinced the Shawnee to turn Kenton over to him so he could be interrogated in Detroit.

In Detroit, Kenton secretly gathered provisions and after months managed to escape. Rather than fleeing south, where the Shawnee would expect him, he moved west to the Wabash through unknown forest and prairie. He returned to Kentucky too late to join George Rogers Clark's initial expedition to capture Illinois from the British, but he along with other Kentuckians joined Clark in Illinois during 1780. Kenton was eager to share with Clark all that he had learned about Detroit, as Clark desired above all else to conquer that British base. Detroit had supplied many raids into Kentucky and threatened both Spanish St. Louis and Clark's own control over Illinois. Kenton's intelligence led Clark to cancel a planned move against Detroit as he realized he lacked sufficient resources to attack the British there with any real chance of success.

Late in 1779, Kenton discovered he had not killed his rival and abandoned the name Simon Butler becoming Simon Kenton once again. In 1780, Kenton met with Clark at Vincennes, but was soon on his way back to Kentucky, bearing a message to Harrodsburg. While there, Boone proposed a raiding party into Shawnee territory to attempt to recover horses taken by the Indians, and of course Kenton joined. The group was discovered and returned, but Kenton and

2. Pierre Drouillard was the father of George Drouillard who served as a hunter on Lewis and Clark's expedition to the Pacific. George Drouillard was killed by the Blackfoot.

Alexander Montgomery stayed behind in an attempt to retrieve some horses. They did get four and returned to Logan's Station. Kenton next went on to scout to the large Shawnee town of Chillicothe. Clark himself was soon back in Kentucky, conducting war against the Shawnee and allied British who had raided and destroyed several settlements. Fighting continued in Kentucky even after the British surrender at Yorktown, and Kenton later recalled proudly that he had served under Clark from 1780 until 1782.

With the end of the Revolution, Kenton gathered a few families who settled with him on Quick's Run in Kentucky. There he had a child, but the mother married one of Kenton's friends rather than Kenton. Kenton soon returned to his old home in Virginia for a visit. There he convinced much of his family to follow him to Kentucky where they could have farms much larger than the tiny plots available to them in Virginia. Indian warfare continued, but a smallpox epidemic swept through the Shawnee, killing hundreds and greatly weakening the tribe.

Kenton, accompanied by many of his relatives from Virginia, settled at Kenton's Station in northern Kentucky, near Washington and not far from the Ohio River. The station was sufficiently strong that it was not subject to attacks by the Shawnee, but the Shawnee did attack individual travelers in the area, isolated cabins, and took horses. Kenton organized his neighbors to oppose these depredations.

Pierre Drouillard, who had saved Kenton from being burned at the stake, came to the station. He had become alcoholic, but Kenton treated him with great kindness, providing housing, food, clothing, and paying for his drink. Drouillard remained with Kenton until his death in 1810.

Bejamin Logan organized a major campaign against the Indians in 1786, and, of course, Kenton participated. The settlers under Logan burned several Indian towns, but within two months, the Shawnee were again raiding in Kentucky. The inhabitants of nearby Washington built a stockade and blockhouse out of fear that a sudden attack would prevent them from fleeing to Kenton Station. Another major campaign against the Indians was organized in 1787, commanded by John Todd and with Kenton as scout. After a successful attack on a major Shawnee camp, peace was made and a general exchange of prisoners arranged. There were false alarms and occasional real incidents in the following years, but the peace held. Simon Kenton married Martha Dowden, much younger than him, that same year. The couple had four children.

In 1788, the area around Kenton Station and Washington became Mason County, named after George Mason, delegate from Virginia to the United States Constitutional Convention, and remembered chiefly for his role in the creation of the Bill of Rights. This new status was an indication of the growing settlement of the area. The 1790 census recorded a population of 2,729 for Mason County. Still, Indians continued to prove a threat to settlers. Black Snake, the Shawnee chief, was again raiding, and Kenton was on his trail. The Indians divided into five groups, each going its own way, but Kenton in an exhibition of superb tracking, was able to discern which group held James Livingston, who had been captured by the Indians. Kenton and his men were able to free the captive.

Kenton took part in General Josiah Harmar's mismanaged campaign, after which Indian raids became more common. After Harmar's campaign, Kenton buried bodies of settlers who had been ambushed and killed while moving goods on Snag Creek. There his men killed six Indians and secured thirty-two horses. Kenton also acted as scout for other expeditions to intercept Indian raiders.

Kenton did not participate in General Arthur St. Clair's disastrous and foolishly blundered campaign in 1791, after which Indian raids into Kentucky increased greatly. When "Mad" Anthony Wayne began his campaign against the tribes centered on the upper Wabash River, Kenton was engaged in a major raid against the Indians who were still attacking in Kentucky. He later joined Wayne's force but fell ill during the winter and had to return home to recuperate, so he was not present at the final battle at Fallen Timbers.

Wayne's campaign, which reached its conclusion in 1794, effectively crippled the tribes and after a few years led to the expulsion of the Native Americans from the Ohio Valley, creating conditions leading to the rapid expansion of settlers to the Mississippi River and beyond.

Engraving of Simon Kenton in old age by Richard W. Dodson, after a painting from life by Louis M. Morgan. (*Kentucky Historical Society*)

The end of Indian raids allowed Kenton to assume a new role, that of benevolent leader of his community. He built a fine brick house, the first of its kind in the area, and there Kenton became fascinated with the acquisition of land, both by claiming previous unsettled areas and by purchase. At one time he owned several thousand acres, and many newcomers to northern Kentucky became tenant farmers on his lands. For rent he took a portion of the crops, but he did not sell the surplus but rather gave it away for free to the poor and needy of the community, and to newcomers who were struggling to establish farms. He even refused payment when it was offered.

In 1796, Simon Kenton's wife died tragically in a house fire, leaving him with four young children. He soon married Elizabeth Jarboe, who like his first wife, was much younger than him. Age disparity in marriage was very common at the time. The couple had six children. Kenton's second wife is described as vivacious and highly intelligent. She wrote down accounts of Kenton's adventures, which he dictated to her. Today, they can be found among the Draper Manuscripts.[3]

3. Draper Manuscript Collection, Series BB; v. 1-13 (OCLC: ocm05913818).

Kenton soon became fascinated with Ohio. In 1799, he and Colonel William Ward led a group of settlers to the area between Springfield and Urbana, Ohio. Kenton simply abandoned much of his land in Kentucky, which reverted to the state for nonpayment of taxes. In 1810, Kenton became a resident of Urbana, in western Ohio, and there he became brigadier general of the state militia. All did not go well for Kenton in Ohio. He made some disastrously bad investments there and in Missouri. In Ohio he got into a dispute over an unpaid debt and was placed under arrest in Urbana for a year before the situation was resolved. He was bailed out and had freedom within the town's limits during that period.

In Missouri, Kenton spent heavily in the purchase of a Spanish grant, but when he lacked the cash for the final payment, he lost the entire investment. He also bought heavily in the town of New Madrid, but in late 1811 and early 1812 New Madrid was struck by the greatest string of earthquakes in the history of the United States. A significant portion of the town and surrounding territory collapsed into the Mississippi River and the rest was destroyed.

Tension with the Indians grew as the Shawnee chief Tecumseh sought to build a coalition of tribes to oppose the increasing flood of settlers, with his brother Tenskwatawa, better known as the Shawnee Prophet, who preached rejection of European influences and reversion to traditional lifestyles. Tenskwatawa founded a multitribal center known as Prophetstown where he preached and gathered his forces. In 1811, as the Midwest became increasingly involved in warfare with the Shawnee and other tribes, US forces commanded by Willian Henry Harrison, were attacked by Tenskwatawa and his followers. After the hard-fought Battle of Tippecanoe, Harrison and his forces destroyed Prophetstown and the crops growing in the area. When the War of 1812 was officially declared, Tecumseh joined the British, who exploited him for their own benefit.

During the War of 1812, Kenton, now in his sixties, served as a scout and commanded a militia unit. He and his unit fought in the Battle of the Thames in which Tecumseh was killed. When Kenton was called upon to identify Tecumseh's body, he realized that soldiers were prepared to mutilate it for souvenirs. Rather than see this happen, Kenton identified another Indian killed in the battle as Tecumseh. Kenton may have fought against Tecumseh, but he respected his foe and saw to it that Tecumseh was respectfully buried.

As Simon Kenton entered his seventies, his wealth was much reduced. He had entrusted others with control of his business matters because he was illiterate. Some had taken advantage of him, and others were simply poor businessmen. He always had enough to live comfortably, but he could no longer make investments in land. Kenton's days of violent conflict were in the past, but he became deeply involved in the local Methodist Church. In 1836, Simon Kenton died. His gravestone bears an epitaph that testifies to his reputation:

> IN
> MEMORY
> OF
> G^{en}. SIMON KENTON
> Who was born April 3rd
> 1755. in Culpepper C$^{o.}$V^{a}
> & Died. April 29. 1836.
> Aged 81 years 26 days.
> His Fellow Citizens of the west,
> Will long remember him, as
> The skilful Pioneer of early
> Times. The brave soldier &
> The honest Man.

Today, Simon Kenton continues to be remembered and honored. In Kentucky, a county, school district, and high school are all named for him. A famous inn is named for him in Springfield, Ohio. He has become the subject of both serious history and imaginative fiction.

CHAPTER THIRTEEN

APEKONIT, THE LINGUISTIC MAN OF VALOR

William Wells

(1770–1812)

William Wells was born in 1770 at Jacob's Creek in southwest Pennsylvania. The family earlier lived in Virginia, where his father, Samuel Wells, served during the American Revolution as a captain in the militia.[1] When William was nine, the family continued their westward movement, migrating to Louisville, Kentucky. William's mother died soon after their arrival. In 1782, Samuel Wells was at Squire Boone's Station, also known as the

1. Harvey Lewis Carter, *The Life and Times of Little Turtle: First Sagamore of the Wabash* (University of Illinois Press, 1987): 82, gives William Wells's father's first name as Hayden rather than Samuel. Other accounts claim that his father's name was Samuel. Confusion may have arisen because an older brother of William's was named Samuel. William Heath, *William Wells and the Struggle for the Old Northwest* (University of Oklahoma Press, 2015), the first study focusing specifically on William Wells, gives the father's name as Samuel, which was also the name of William's grandfather.

Painted Stone Station, which was primarily a defensive settlement although some trading took place. As Indian warfare became more threating, the inhabitants of the station sought to evacuate, but they were attacked by Miami warriors over two days. During the fighting on the second day, Samuel Wells was killed. After the death of his father, William went to live with Colonel William Pope.

In 1784, when William was thirteen, he and three other boys were captured in a raid by Miami Indians, perhaps joined by some Delaware (Lenape). The three other boys went to the Delaware tribe but were able to escape after a short time. William was adopted by a Miami chief and lived at the Miami village on the Eel River throughout his teen years. William had red hair and was named Apekonit, which means "carrot" in the Miami language, and would seem to be an obvious reference to his hair color. William seems to have adapted to life among the Miami easily and married a Wea woman and had a daughter by her. The Wea were a subdivision of the Miami people. In 1791, William's wife and child were captured in a raid commanded by General James Wilkinson and imprisoned in Cincinnati.

While his first wife was held captive, Apekonit, the name under which he was living and functioning, married a daughter of the Miami leader Little Turtle, by whom he had four children. Wells's relationship with Little Turtle puzzled many whites, and some hypothesized a "family compact," by which each swore not to kill the other in battle. The "family compact," however, remains more a matter of speculation than fact.

Apekonit did not hesitate to fight for the Miami. At the great victory of the Miami and other tribes over General St. Clair in 1791, Apekonit commanded a group of Miami marksmen who did important service during the battle. They shot down St. Clair's cannoneers, limiting their role in the battle.[2] Some artillery was brought into action, but it proved ineffective, firing cannister and round shot into heavy forest, damaging trees but causing few casualties. St. Clair's

2. Winkler, John F., *Wabash 1791: St. Clair's Defeat*, Osprey Campaign Series #240 (Osprey Publishing, 2011), 65. [SCHOENFIELD]

defeat, largely brought about by his own arrogance and having underestimated his opponents, was the greatest Indian victory over a United States army which suffered the greatest loss of life in a battle until the Civil War.

Even while living among the Miami, Wells did not entirely lose contact with his original family. His brother Cary visited him at Eel River in the late 1780s, and in 1792, while attempting to find a way to free the prisoners at Cincinnati, William met with his brother Sam at Louisville. Sam encouraged William to travel to Cincinnati to meet Rufus Putnam. Putnam had fought in the French and Indian War and served as a brigadier general during the American Revolution. After the war he became a chief organizer in the Ohio Company of Associates, which played a major role in promoting settlers to move into the Ohio Territory. In 1788, Putnam led a settlement of Revolutionary War veterans who settled by the confluence of the Ohio and Muskingum Rivers, in modern-day Marietta, Ohio. This was the first permanent settler community established in the Northwest Territory. Putnam served as a brigadier general under the command of Anthony Wayne during the Ohio campaign in 1792 and 1793. From 1796 until 1803, Putnam served as the first surveyor general of the United States.

Putnam wished to make a treaty with tribes and hired Wells to assist him. Although not the intent, Wells's association with Putnam facilitated his return to the world of settlers and enrollment in the United States army. There was some risk for Wells in going to the Miami for Putnam, as it was apparent to the Miami that Wells was beginning to defect from the tribe. Putnam paid Wells handsomely. He received $300, a significant sum at the time, in an attempt to persuade the Miami and the Delaware of White River to participate in peace talks.

In 1792, Putnam successfully negotiated a peace treaty with several of the Wabash tribes, which was signed by thirty-one chiefs. As part of the treaty, prisoners were released, but by an overwhelming vote the Senate failed to ratify the treaty so the conflict between the tribes and the United States army continued. Wells had not lost all credibility with the Indians, and so Putnam was able to hire Wells to report on the councils held among the tribes along the Maumee River.[3]

Wells was a remarkable linguist, speaking at least five different Indian dialects and generally thought to be the most fluent speaker of Native tongues in the Midwest. Anthony Wayne, commissioned to do what St. Clair had failed, also recognized that Wells was familiar with the territory in which he would be operating and knew the Indian leaders and their tactics. He recruited Wells and gave him the honorary rank of captain of the scouts, marking his complete break with the Miami and his return to Anglo-American society. Wells served faithfully but was wounded shortly before Fallen Timbers and so did not participate in that battle. More than the famous battle at Fallen Timbers, Wayne's scorched earth policy, burning Indian towns and crops, was responsible for displacing the Indians of the upper Wabash River region and opening the territory for new Anglo-American settlers.[4]

After Wayne's campaign, Wells served as an interpreter for the Indians on the upper Wabash at the Treaty of Greenville, by which the defeated Indians ceded most of Ohio. Little Turtle, Wells's father-in-law, requested that Wells be appointed as Indian agent at Fort Wayne. Wells also traveled to Philadelphia with Little Turtle to meet with President George Washington, and then in 1797, the two traveled again to meet with the new president, John Adams. Nothing of great significance came out of either meeting.

When Thomas Jefferson became president, Wells requested that a government trading post be established at Fort Wayne. The post was established but John Johnston was appointed as manager rather than Wells, who was retained in the post of Indian agent. Johnston and Wells did not work well together, and Wells fell out of favor with the territorial governor William Henry Harrison. In 1805,

3. Carter, *The Life and Times*, 82–86 and 112–37, provides a good overview of Wells reintegration into white society.

4. For recent and comprehensive treatments of Antony Wayne, see Mary Stockwell, *Unlikely General: "Mad" Anthony Wayne and the Battle for America* (Yale University Press, 2018) and William Hogeland, *Autumn of the Black Snake* (Farrar, Straus and Giroux, 2018).

Portrait of William Wells by an unknown artist. (*Chicago History Museum*)

Harrison instituted an investigation of Wells on charges of fiscal corruption by profiting from contracts for the trading post and supporting the Miami in preference to settlers. The investigation concluded that Wells did tend to favor Indians above settlers. That same year, Wells's Miami wife died and in 1809 he married again, the daughter of an army colonel. In 1808, Wells led a group of Indian chiefs from several tribes to Washington, DC, to meet with President Jefferson. Secretary of War Henry Dearborn felt going directly to the president subverted the chain of command and fired Wells as Indian agent, putting John Johnston in his place. Wells remained at Fort Wayne as translator of Indian languages. Wells in partnership with Jean-François Hamtramck briefly tried his hand at farming but continued his service in the army.

Late in the first decade of the nineteenth century, Tecumseh and his brother Tenskwatawa, the Shawnee prophet, became prominent, and Wells attempted to warn Washington of this growing threat of the brothers having drawn remarkable attention and that they were becoming well known. Consequently, Tecumseh, his brother, and their followers considered Wells an enemy. The US government largely ignored Wells's warning.

In 1811, relations between various Indian groups and settlers in Illinois deteriorated and violent confrontations took place. Fort Dearborn, located near the center of what is now Chicago, was an isolated Indian trading "factory," so called because it was run by a government appointed "factor." The nearest post was Fort Wayne, about 166 miles away. Fort Dearborn, founded in 1803, was not a happy post. In addition to isolation, the officers there had so fallen into quarreling that in 1810 the commander and other senior officers were removed and replaced by others. While the factory had been established to counter British influence and to trade peacefully with the Potawatomi, it failed to achieve those aims. The Potawatomi were agitated by settlers entering Illinois, by the preachings of Tecumseh and his brother Tenskwatawa, and by British incitements.

The commanding officer at Fort Wayne ordered Fort Dearborn to be evacuated and the people there to withdraw to Fort Wayne. The orders were received at Fort Dearborn on August 9, 1812, but unfortunately the fort was occupied within a week. The post commander Nathan Heald had ordered that goods that could not be carried away should be given to the local Indians, but he decided that it would be too risky to give the Indians the post's supply of alcohol and ammunition, and had both destroyed, which infuriated the Indians. While the inhabitants of the fort arranged the evacuation, the Potawatomi debated whether to remain neutral or attack the evacuees. Those allied with the British and Tecumseh and those hostile to the United States prevailed. William Wells arrived on August 13 accompanied by about thirty Miami to aid in the departure.

The evacuation began about 9:00 a.m. on August 15, 1812.[5] The number of people leaving Fort Dearborn is uncertain, but there were about fifty-four officers and enlisted men, nine women, eighteen children, and twelve militiamen. The thirty Miami came at the end of

5. There are many accounts of the Fort Dearborn Massacre. See, Gillum Ferguson, *Illinois in the War of 1812* (University of Illinois Press, 2012), 66–67, which provides a reliable account.

the column as they moved south paralleling the shore of Lake Michigan, and Wells was mounted on a horse and thought to have ridden at or near the head of the group. Wells was certain that the Potawatomi would attack the column of evacuees and that he would die in the subsequent fight. Reverting to a practice common among Indians, Wells painted his face black, a sign of his acceptance of his fate.

The column covered only about a mile and a half when the Potawatomi, numbering as many as five hundred, attacked from behind some dunes that had concealed them. The assault was overwhelming and about fifty-three men, several women, and many of the children were killed. According to reports, Wells was among the first killed. Regarded as an enemy by Tecumseh and the Shawnee prophet, he attracted much gun fire. The survivors of the assault, some wounded, surrendered, and some more were killed even after the surrender. The victorious Potawatomi burned Fort Dearborn. Potawatomi who had opposed the attack intervened to protect and save a few of the prisoners.

The Potawatomi may have regarded Wells as a traitor to the Indian cause, but they honored his courage. They opened his chest and removed his heart, which they cut into many pieces, giving each warrior a small piece to consume in order to gain Wells's valor.

William Wells was a man of two worlds. He passed his childhood as the son of a white settler and then his formative teenage years as a Miami Indian warrior. When he was a little more than twenty years old circumstances led to his return to white society, but that reintegration was never complete. He served as a captain of scouts under Anthony Wayne, and after that remained in the United States Army, but he was accused of favoring Indians over settlers and deprived of his position as Indian agent. He subsequently spent years as a mere translator of Indian languages at Fort Wayne. Wells was sent to Fort Dearborn to aid in the evacuation, and while there he realized that the Potawatomi would attack the evacuees, and he foresaw his own death. The circumstances of his death at the Fort Dearborn Massacre testify to the deep, lasting influences of his years as a member of the Miami.

CHAPTER FOURTEEN

EARLY MOUNTAIN MAN

John Colter

(ca. 1770/1775–ca. 1812/1813)

There is no documentary evidence about the origins of John Colter. Eva Emery Dye, who wrote an idealized account of the Lewis and Clark Expedition, also wrote a detailed account of Colter's background, but she made no references to any documentary sources. The following narrative, though often accepted and repeated, must be regarded as highly dubious. John Colter was supposedly born sometime between 1770 and 1775, most likely in 1774, at Stuarts Draft in north central Virginia.[1] His family was of Scottish origin, but like many others they had migrated first to Ireland, and then eventually to America. The family name seems

1. Eva Emery Dye, the author of *The Conquest: The True Story of Lewis and Clark* (McClurg, 1903), a greatly idealized and romanticized account, made claims about the origins and parentage of Colter, but the statements lack all documentation. Similarly, Dye made many claims about Sacagawea that are entirely without substantiation, though they have contributed much to her reputation. Dye's fables have been repeated because of the lack of any other accounts. Ron Anglin and Larry E. Morris, *Gloomy Terrors*

to have been originally spelled Coalter, possibly indicating that they worked in coal mining or coal processing. Colter may have gotten his first wilderness experience serving as a ranger under the command of Simon Kenton during Lord Dunmore's War, but documentary evidence is again lacking. Ron Anglin and Larry E. Morris summed up succinctly what is really known about John Colter before the Lewis and Clark Expedition: nothing. Even Colter's enrollment in the expedition on October 15, 1803, is hardly secure. No notation of the event was made that day; his enlistment was only recorded in 1807 by Clark in St. Louis, months after the end of the expedition. It is not even certain whether Colter was literate. At least he could sign his name, which he wrote as "John Colter." He did not record his own adventures, but fortunately others did.

In Lewis's journal, Colter's name also appears as Coalter and Coulter. Such variations in the spelling of names were common in the period, especially in Lewis's journal, which is distinguished by the originality of his English. During the training of new recruits in the winter of 1803–1804, Colter and a few friends got themselves in a bit of trouble. They went hunting but ended up in a whiskey shop. For this, Colter and the others were confined to camp for ten days.

and Hidden Fires: The Mystery of John Colter and Yellowstone (Rowman & Littlefield, 2014): 9–12, offers a clear critique of Dye's unsubstantiated stories about Colter.

Much has been written about John Colter, including Stallo Vinton's *The Biography of John Colter: The Discoverer of Yellowstone Park* (Edw. Eberstadt, New York, 1926). This work by Vinton is the earliest good biography of Colter. It is short but remains of interest. It has frequently been 'reprinted,' most recently by Rowman and Littlefield, in 2014. Also noteworthy is Mary Blount Christian and Laszlo Kubinyi, *Who'd Believe John Colter?* (Maxwell Macmillan International, 1993); Stephen T. Gough and Gale Gough, *Colter's Run* (Falcon Press, 1993); Burton Harris, *John Colter, His Years in the Rockies* (University of Nebraska Press, 1993); Robert M. Utley, *A Life Wild and Perilous: Mountain Men and the Paths to the Pacific* (Henry Holt and Co., 1998); Don Amiet, *John Colter: The Legend of the First Mountain Man* (PublishAmerica, 2009); Win Blevins, *The First Mountain Man: John Colter* (PublishAmerica, 2009). Anglin and Morris's *Gloomy Terrors* (2014) examines Colter's life in detail and contains transcriptions of many important documents, including the various accounts of Colter's Run, and an excellent account of all the documentation concerning Colter.

As the Lewis and Clark expedition moved west, John Colter and George Drouillard were detailed to serve as hunters, a highly responsible position, to bring fresh meat to the company. The hunter had to find game, field dress it, and then catch up to the main body of the expedition that had, of course, continued its trek westward. The journals of Lewis and Clark bear many favorable references to Colter. After reaching the Pacific and spending a gloomy, rainy winter there, the Corps of Discovery headed back to St. Louis. At the villages of the Mandan, Colter met two men who were headed for the mountains to trap beaver. He requested and received an early discharge from the expedition. This was a very unusual procedure, and Lewis and Clark make it apparent it was only granted to Colter because of his exemplary service.

The partnership did not endure, and Colter set out on his own in the spring. He soon encountered a party of trappers headed by Manuel Lisa. The group included several veterans of the Corps of Discovery who were familiar to Colter, and Lisa persuaded Colter to join his expedition. That was to the advantage of both. Lisa benefitted from Colter's knowledge of the land, while Colter could bring his pelts to Lisa and trade them for the ammunition, gunpowder, traps, and other equipment he needed without having to travel all the way down to St. Louis for resupply.

After Lisa established Fort Raymond, named after his son, Colter was sent out to bring word to the Crow tribe and any other Indians he might encounter, that Lisa's fort was open for trade. The noted mountain man George Drouillard also spread the word of Lisa's trading post. Colter, alone and carrying a rifle and thirty-pound pack covered about five hundred miles in the wilderness. His exact route cannot be traced, but apparently he was the first non-native to reach Jackson Hole, the valley between the Gros Ventre and Teton mountain ranges in Wyoming near the Idaho border. He also seems to have reached the north edge of Yellowstone Lake. He certainly did not see the major geyser basins and may not have seen even one geyser—the assertion that he did may be a later accretion to the story. Colter definitely did see boiling springs surrounded by multicolored mats of bacteria, bubbling mud pots, and he reported the pervasive smell of sulfur in the air. Colter's accounts of the wonders he had encountered were widely disbelieved and his stories were called jokingly "Colter's Hell," as if he had seen a divine vision of the inferno as a warning. Subsequent discoveries proved his accounts true.

Later, while moving with a group of Flathead Indians toward Lisa's post, Colter and the others were ambushed by Blackfoot Indians. Fortunately, a nearby body of Crow intervened on the side of Colter and the Flathead, driving off the Blackfoot. During the affray, Colter was shot in the leg. He recuperated at Fort Raymond, and in the autumn of 1808, he set out to trap along with John Potts. Traveling on what would come to be called the Jefferson River, Colter and Potts, each with his own canoe, suddenly found themselves confronted with several hundred Blackfoot warriors. They ordered the trappers to come to shore. Colter dropped his traps in the river and came to the riverside, while Potts held back. On shore, the Indians stripped Colter naked, and one shot at and wounded Potts. Potts fired back, killing an Indian. The mass of warriors fired on Potts, killing him instantly.[2] Colter expected to be slaughtered, but the Blackfoot told him to go. Colter immediately realized they intended to have him run for his life, to be chased by a group of warriors with homicidal intent.

Thus began "Colter's Run," one of the most storied events of the early wilderness. Colter was a swift runner. He headed for the Madison River, about five miles distant, crossing a plain covered by prickly pear cactus, the needles of which stuck in his feet. As Colter ran, his nose began to bleed from the exertion, covering his lower face and chest in red. He soon outdistanced all but one warrior who was only about twenty paces behind him when Colter turned to confront the man. Startled, the warrior hesitated and stumbled when he attempted to throw his spear at Colter. The spear broke, and Colter was able to grasp the sharp end, with which he stabbed the Indian to death, seized a blanket from the man, and ran on with it and the

2. Accounts vary whether Potts was killed by bullets or arrows.

broken spear. Colter managed to reach the river, dove in, and swam to hide under a log jam.[3] The Indians searched upstream and downstream for signs of Colter and even walked across the log jam. Colter feared the Indians would set the log jam on fire, something they were known to do. Later that night he swam downstream underwater, surfacing only when necessary. Colter feared the Blackfoot would be waiting where the river narrowed, so he left it, climbing a very steep slope clinging to rocks and plants. The Indians eventually gave up searching for him, but he was naked and barefooted and had nothing but the stolen blanket and the broken spear. Over the next eleven days,[4] Colter traveled about 235 miles through mountainous country, resting seldom and then only briefly, eating only a few roots. He finally stumbled into Lisa's Fort Raymond, where he was not recognizable until he made himself known. There he recuperated from his ordeal.

After recovering, Colter set out to retrieve the traps he had dumped in the river. Camping on a bank of the Gallatin River, he was ambushed one night, but his acute senses detected sounds of Indians approaching his camp, and he managed to escape into the darkness as bullets riddled his camp. Although his friend George Drouillard was not with him at that time, Colter was to later learn that Drouillard's end had been quite sad, as he was not so lucky. He too had been ambushed, but after a spirited defense he was killed, and his body mutilated.

In 1810, after six years in the wilderness, Colter traveled to St. Louis, where among other things he collected his wages from the Lewis and Clark Expedition. Colter collaborated with Clark, then a high government official, to produce a map of the area in which he traveled. The map was inaccurate in many details, but it was the best that would be produced for decades.

3. Accounts vary, some claiming that Colter found refuge in a beaver's den rather than a log jam. The story of the beaver's den seems much less likely. The Indians would surely have known about the architecture of a beaver's den and the potential for hiding there.

4. Some accounts say only seven days, but that seems little time to cover about 235 miles barefoot in the mountains.

Colter decided, after his close escapes and the death of Drouillard, that it was time to retire from beaver trapping. He married and purchased a farm near Miller's Landing in Missouri, but during the War of 1812 he joined Nathan Boone's Rangers. The date and cause of his death are as uncertain as his birth. One account claims he died in mid-1812 of jaundice while another indicates he died in late 1813. He was only about thirty-nine or forty years old, but early death was not unusual in the nineteenth century.

John Colter is generally credited with being the first of the mountain men, though others such as George Drouillard, the unfortunate John Potts, and other trappers might equally claim the same title. His explorations and tales of his discoveries, later confirmed, certainly contributed to his notoriety. Along with others such as Drouillard and Lisa, he helped explore and open the northern territory of the Missouri and nearby rivers, which proved valuable in the eventual determination of the northern border of the United States.

CHAPTER FIFTEEN

FUR TRADER EXTRAORDINAIRE

Manuel Lisa

(1772–1820)

MANUEL LISA was probably born at New Orleans in 1772, the son of Christoval de Lisa of Murcia, Spain, and Maria Ignacia Rodriguez of St. Augustine, Florida.[1] At the time, Spain controlled "the isle" of New Orleans and what had been French territory west of the Mississippi. The territory had been ceded to Spain by France at the end of the Seven Years War, called the French and Indian War by English colonists. Lisa's father seems to have served as a middle-ranking Spanish governmental bureaucrat. It is

1. It is possible that Lisa was born in Cuba or elsewhere in the Caribbean, and his date of birth may not have been 1772 as recorded on his grave. In a letter, he referred to his brother Joaquin as older (Manuel Lisa to William Clark, July 1, 1817, printed in the *Missouri Gazette* of July 5, 1817), but Joaquin's birth certificate from New Orleans gives his birth date as December 21, 1774. Of course, a transcription error in copying the letter cannot be ruled out entirely. In 1804, Joaquin moved back to New Orleans permanently. The best book on Manuel Lisa is Richard E. Oglesby's, *Manuel Lisa and the Opening of the Missouri Fur Trade* (Oklahoma University Press, 1963), see also Hiram

likely that Lisa's father came to New Orleans along with Governor Alejandro O' Reilly, who was sent to New Orleans to suppress ill-conceived French opposition to Spanish rule. O' Reilly did just that by hanging several ringleaders, despite their high social standing.

Little is known of Lisa's early years. It is apparent he received a good basic education. He was fully literate and capable of maintaining complex business records. Personally, Lisa seems to have had compassion for women and children, but he was fiercely competitive with other men. Always active and quick to embrace new ideas, he was also confrontational, litigious, and quarrelsome. Nominally Catholic, he could be conventionally religious when an occasion required, but religion seems to have occupied a minor part of his life.

In 1796, Manuel was already engaged in trade along with his older brother Joaquin, moving goods on the Mississippi River from New Orleans to New Madrid, Missouri. He also established a store at Vincennes and traded on the Wabash River. Also, in or about 1796, Manuel had married a young widow from New Orleans, Polly C. Chew, who had a sickly daughter. Her husband had been killed by Indians and Polly and her daughter Rachael had been held captive until ransomed. Manuel Lisa and his bride Polly eventually had two boys, Raymond and Manuel. In 1797, Lisa was in Cincinnati purchasing goods to trade at Vincennes. By 1799, he moved his family to St. Louis, which had become the center of the fur trade, eclipsing Kaskaskia in Illinois. There he opened a store in St. Louis and shipped goods to New Madrid, Ste. Genevieve, and Vincennes.

By 1799, Lisa encountered a significant problem as he attempted to grow his business. The Spanish government awarded monopolies for trade with specific tribes. Auguste and Pierre Chouteau held the richest monopoly for trade with the Osage, while other merchants held monopolies for trade with different tribes. As monopolies were

Martin Chittenden, *The American Fur Trade of the Far West* (F. P. Harper Co., 1902); Herbert Eugene Bolton,"New Light on Manuel Lisa and the Spanish Fur Trade,"*The Southwestern Historical Quarterly* 17, no. 1 (July 1913): 61–66; Cardinal Goodwin, "Manuel Lisa," *The Overland Monthly* 68, no. 2 (February 1917): 151–55; Walter B. Douglas, *Manuel Lisa*, ed. Abraham Phineas Nasatir (Argosy-Antiquarian, 1964).

normally granted for a period of years, it was virtually impossible for new merchants to break into the privileged group that held such licenses. Lisa, always active and frequently litigious, drew up a petition arguing the virtues of free trade. He persuaded others to add their endorsements to the petition, including even some who held monopolies to trade with specific tribes. He presented this document to the lieutenant governor of Upper Louisiana, Charles Dehault Delassus, who quickly rejected it.[2] Lisa brought the petition to New Orleans and requested it be brought to the attention of the king and his council, but again it was rejected. The Spanish government was content with the current situation and wished no unnecessary disruption.

There was another reason Lisa's petition was rejected, one that he could not have known, and which may have been unknown even to the governor in New Orleans. Spain was about to sign a secret treaty with France, the Treaty of San Ildefonso. In 1800, Napoleon virtually annexed Italy, and Spain agreed to a secret treaty by which it agreed to retrocede Louisiana to France in exchange for existing Spanish dynastic claims in Italy. Spain had no desire to implement new measures in territory it would soon loose. The Spanish government delayed implementing the treaty until 1802, and it was not until 1804 that Spanish control of Louisiana ended. France, confounded by Britain's dominance on the seas and the formation of the Second Coalition, quickly sold the Louisiana Territory, all the French holdings west of the Mississippi River, and the "isle" of New Orleans, to the United States.

If Lisa could not get free trade, he would break into the circle of those who had monopolies, and he intended to take the Osage trade away from the Chouteaus. Lisa formed a company with Francisco Maria Benoît, Carlos Sanguinet, and Gregorio Sarpy. The company was known simply as Manuel Lisa, Benoît, and Company. There was much clandestine trade across the Mississippi with the Americans in Cahokia, particularly as the Americans were able to produce a

2. For Charles Dehault Delassus and his family see Carl J. Ekberg, *A French Aristocrat in the American West: The Shattered Dreams of De Lassus De Luzières* (University of Missouri Press, 2010).

popular flour superior to that milled in St. Louis. Lisa and his associates promised to build a milling facility that would make smuggling unnecessary and also gift a thousand pesos to the royal treasury. One wonders if the gift made it to the treasury. This was sufficient for the governor in New Orleans to cancel the Chouteaus's monopoly and reward Lisa and Company with the monopoly of trade with the Osage of Missouri, although the Chouteaus continued to hold the right to supply the garrison at the Osage fort.

The Chouteaus were also not above a little illegal trading, particularly regarding alcohol. Lisa and associates captured a boat belonging to the Chouteaus loaded with liquor intended for sale to soldiers and Indians. Lisa complained to Lieutenant Governor Delassus, but when he took no action, Lisa wrote an intemperate denunciation. Delassus had Lisa imprisoned, and Lisa wrote an apology for any personal insult, but that only resulted in Lisa being moved from jail to house arrest. The matter was brought to the attention of Governor Manuel Juan de Salcedo in New Orleans, who approved of Delassus's actions, but Lisa was released from house arrest. Still, the conflict with the Chouteaus was not over.

The Chouteaus cleverly persuaded a large group of Osage to move from Missouri to Arkansas, thus beyond the monopoly of Manuel Lisa, Benoît, and Company. This severely limited the profit from the Osage trade. When construction began on the flour mill, Lisa was short of cash and so took out a loan of 1,500 pesos in the name of the company. The Chouteaus bought the debt, and when it came due sought to collect from Lisa, who was still short of cash and could not pay. The other partners were able to pay their share of the debt, but Lisa insisted on going to trial. The day the Chouteaus pressed their case was the day that France sold the Louisiana Territory, including St. Louis, to the United States. Profound changes would follow. The Chouteaus were eventually paid, but their relations with Lisa remained strained.

The American acquisition of the Louisiana Territory was quickly followed by President Jefferson's plan to have Meriwether Lewis, formerly the presidential secretary, and William Clark, former soldier and member of a prominent Virginia family, to create the Corps of

Discovery for crossing the American continent. The plan was to follow the Missouri River to its source, then cross the Rocky Mountains, and proceed to the Pacific Ocean. The Corps would require a variety of supplies, some in quantity. Lewis and Clark went to the Chouteaus, to Manuel Lisa, and to other merchants. The attraction of Lisa's store was the great variety of goods available there. At first, the explorers got on well with Lisa, but relations deteriorated. A letter in the William Clark Collection in the National Archives contains the following:

> Damn Manuel and triple damn Mr. B. [Benoit] They give me more vexation than their lives are worth—I have dealt very plainly with these gentlemen, in short I have come to an open rupture with them; I think them both great scoundrels.[3]

The disillusionment did not last. Later, Clark was a business partner of Lisa, and Lewis became a patron of Lisa's Missouri Fur Company. Lisa also provided food and housing for Spanish soldiers until they could be transported to Spanish territory, for a fee of course. The transfer was long delayed, from March to October, which undoubtedly proved beneficial to Lisa's bank account.

The Louisiana Purchase opened new opportunities for Manuel Lisa. There were no more monopolies, but the lieutenant governor issued licenses, designed to prevent conflict. There was much speculation in St. Louis about Lisa's intensions, most supposing that he intended to open trade with the Spanish at Santa Fe. Lisa did have some interest in Spanish trade, but so did many others. The royal Spanish government, however, consistently opposed any trade between foreign colonies, seeking a pure mercantilist relation with the colonies, where all raw resources flowed from the colonies to Spain and the colonies purchased all manufactured and processed materials from Spain.

3. Meriwether Lewis to William Clark, December 17, 1803, quoted in Oglesby, *Manuel Lisa*, 30.

Lisa spent much of 1805 and early 1806 involved in court cases, attempting to collect outstanding debts, but by mid-1806, he had formulated new plans. He established a partnership with two of the most important men in Illinois, Pierre Menard and William Morrison, both of Kaskaskia. Rather than trade with Santa Fe, the partners sought beaver pelts from the headwaters of the Missouri River. The men from Kaskaskia invested their money; Lisa arranged the expedition, which consisted of two keelboats manned by fifty to sixty men, many of whom had served on Lewis and Clark's expedition. The keelboats carried $16,000 worth of trade goods. Lisa intended to ascend the Missouri River to the Rocky Mountains, where beaver pelts were reputed to be readily available for trade. The expedition departed in the spring of 1807 amidst widespread predictions that they were heading for disaster.

The Missouri is a difficult river, running normally at about four miles an hour in the main channel. The muddy Missouri has famously been described as too thin to plow and too thick to drink. The river frequently carried entire trees, and snags, trees one end of which had become anchored in the riverbed, bobbing menacingly. Either could hole and sink a keelboat. Additionally, banks sometimes collapsed, and the river could suddenly rise from rainfall upstream. Promising channels might suddenly end in enormous logjams, requiring boats to retreat to another channel to proceed upstream. Moving the keelboats upriver required unending labor, whether using poles, cordelles, or paddles.

There were one or two desertions, but the expedition was more than compensated by the encounter with François Le Compt and John Colter, both very knowledgeable about the area to which they were traveling. Both agreed to join the expedition. By the time the company reached the vicinity of the Platte River, their supplies were largely consumed, and hunting was poor. Food had to be rationed. Two groups of Indians, the Arikara and Assiniboine, showed themselves initially hostile to Lisa and his men, while the Mandan, generally peaceful and cooperative, were unusually truculent. Lisa was consistently bold and steady in his approach and emerged peacefully from the confrontations.

Map of North America, published in 1804, showing the newly acquired Louisiana Territory. (*Library of Congress*)

Pierre Chouteau Jr. coming upriver with a small group of twenty-three men, to convey a Mandan chief back to his home village, did not fare so well. The Arikara, also called the Rees, attacked the group, killing four and wounding more. The Chouteau's group returned to St. Louis without bringing the Mandan chief home, and almost predictably, Pierre Chouteau Jr. sought to blame the disaster on Manuel Lisa. In a report to the secretary of war, Clark praised Chouteau but placed the ultimate blame for the hostilities on the British. Lisa would eventually bring the chief back to his people.

The Lisa contingent continued upstream until they reached the Yellowstone River, which they followed until they reached the confluence with the Bighorn River, where they decided to spend the winter. Hunting there was better. They founded Fort Raymond, named after Lisa's son as a trading post, and built cabins for the winter. As winter set in, John Colter undertook a tour of the area to inform the local Indians that the post was open for trading, and he made another similar trip in the spring. Lisa traded beaver pelts with the Crow, and also trappers belonging to a group who had brought in a harvest of abundant beaver pelts from the area. Returning to St. Louis, the trading expedition was a great success and produced a good profit, but perhaps more importantly, Lisa had opened the upper Missouri to exploration. Others had either to copy Lisa's achievement or find themselves left behind by the competition.

When Lisa returned to St. Louis, he was greeted but not in the way he had anticipated. He, along with his faithful assistant George Drouillard, were put on trial for murder. On the way up the Missouri River, near the mouth of the Osage River, Antoine Bissonette deserted Lisa's expedition. Bissonette had signed a contract to serve for three years, and like most other men he had received an advance on his wages so he could take care of matters before departing. Lisa was outraged by the desertion, and he dispatched George Drouillard to bring Bissonette back. In doing so, he uttered fateful words, telling Drouillard to bring the deserter back dead or alive. When Drouillard caught Bissonette there was a confrontation. Drouillard shot Bissonette and hauled him, severely wounded, back to Lisa. Lisa put Bissonette in a canoe and sent him with men to St. Charles, near St. Louis, for medical attention, but Bissonette died before reaching the town. During the trial it became apparent that Bissonette had long planned his desertion, planting caches of equipment to facilitate his plan. Traders had no sympathy for anyone who took an advance of wages and planned to desert. The jury took fifteen minutes to render a decision of not guilty for both men.

While the expedition of 1807–1808 had been profitable, Lisa realized that to harvest the full potential of the upper Missouri region would require a much greater investment than the initial $16,000 of the initial venture. This was the genesis of the Missouri Fur Company, one of whose investors, despite earlier annoyance, was William Clark. In 1807, President Thomas Jefferson appointed Clark brigadier general of the militia for the Louisiana Territory and federal Indian agent. In 1813, President James Monroe appointed Clark as territorial governor of Missouri, a post he held until 1820. Other investors included James Wilkinson (then territorial governor), Pierre Menard, William Morrison, and, perhaps surprisingly, members of the Chouteau family: Jean Pierre (son of René Auguste) and his son Auguste Pierre, as well as other prominent and wealthy inhabitants of St. Louis. Over the years, the company would dissolve and reform after expeditions, finally enduring until 1830, by which time changes in style, the declining number of beavers, and competition from John Jacob Astor made it no longer profitable.

The initial agreement was to last for three years, and the elaborate regulations about voting, expenditure of money, and distribution of income made it apparent that there was little trust among the investors. Such rules, sometimes at the cost of efficient administration, were nevertheless common in contemporary partnerships.

The expedition, which left St. Louis in the spring of 1809, was much larger than the previous group, numbering about 350 men including a mixture of Americans and French creoles and a few Lenape (Delaware) and Shawnee who were to serve as hunters to bring in fresh meat. The group was accommodated on the trip up the Missouri River in thirteen keelboats and barges. There were some desertions and discontent, chiefly among the Americans who were not used to the laborious dawn to dusk exertions of moving the boats upstream. Progress upriver was predictably slow, but the men grew accustomed to the labor, and leaders began to emerge among them.

As they proceeded upriver, matters became more complex. While the men constructed Fort Mandan as a trading post, a point from which beaver trappers could proceed into the countryside on land, word came that the British had constructed a fort at the three forks of the Missouri. The Blackfoot were unfriendly, casting doubt on the report of the British fort.

John Colter then stumbled into camp. He had been trapping with John Potts when suddenly confronted with five or six hundred Blackfoot. Potts was killed and Colter made to run for his life while chased by angry Indians. "Colter's Run" has become one of the classic stories of the wilderness. He escaped the Indians and arrived at Fort

Raymond after traveling naked and barefoot for about 235 miles in eleven days, living on a few roots.[4]

Pierre Menard went up the Missouri with the expedition, and he managed matters as best he could after Chouteau and Lisa returned to St. Louis to deal with matters there. It was not easy in the face of Americans grumbling and Blackfoot hostility. The trappers established Fort Henry, also known as Henry's Fort, on the Three Forks. It was named after the popular Andrew Henry, second-in-command after Pierre Menard. The Blackfoot killed at least seven trappers including two Shawnee, and several more trappers disappeared. Among those killed was George Drouillard. It did not take Menard long to realize he did not relish the life of a mountain man. In July of 1810, he returned to his pleasant home, which still exists and may be visited, just across the Mississippi from the site of Kaskaskia, washed away by a change in the course of the river.[5] Despite the disappointing Blackfoot hostility and various conflicts, the expedition turned a profit, though not as much as the organizers had hoped and expected. Menard felt that while beavers were truly abundant in the area, nothing could be permanently established unless the Blackfoot could be destroyed, or peace could be made with them. The Blackfoot were, however, not amenable to offers of peace, particularly as the British supplied them with various goods and also encouraged their anger toward non-native Americans.

In 1812, the Missouri Fur Company was reorganized in a new, somewhat more efficient form. No longer were all partners expected to go upcountry to participate in the firm. Several other factors changed. William Morrison quarreled with Lisa and no longer took part in the company. John Jacob Astor sent his first expedition to the upper Missouri. He would be a fierce competitor, but at times

4. See chapter 14 of this volume.

5. For the fate of Kaskaskia, see David MacDonald and Raine Waters, *Kaskaskia: The Lost Capital of Illinois* (Southern Illinois University Press, 2019). The Kaskaskia that tourists may now visit is New Kaskaskia, founded in the 1890s as the last of old Kaskaskia was washed away by the Mississippi. For Pierre Menard in the mountains, see Richard Edward Oglesby, "Pierre Menard, Reluctant Mountain Man," *Bulletin of the Missouri Historical Society* 24, no.1 (October 1967): 3–19.

Astor's men and the Missouri Fur Company would cooperate. Tensions between the British and the United States were increasing and would soon result in the War of 1812. The British encouraged the Sioux and other tribes to become hostile to Americans. The Missouri Fur Company expedition of 1812, commanded by Lisa, was much smaller than the massive effort of 1809–1810, and it was at least in part an effort to relieve trappers who had been left upriver. When reached, the trappers had tales of extreme hardships during the winter, but they also brought many packs of beaver pelts.

In 1812, the original organization of the Missouri Fur Company expired, and it was reorganized as a limited liability partnership, run by a board of three directors: William Clark, Manuel Lisa, and Sylvestre Labbadie, who had long been associated with the company. Stock shares were available for $1,000 each with profits divided annually, and a stockholders meeting was scheduled for the first Monday in December each year. The company would dissolve in 1818. One director would go upriver every year to command the expedition. Since Lisa was well-known and respected by the Indians for his honesty, he was always chosen to command the traders. He also determined which goods to ship up the Missouri and in what quantities.

As Britain and the United States went to war, credit disappeared in St. Louis. Merchants were afraid, rightly, that Britain would do its best to incite the Indians and the upper Missouri would become a battle ground rather than an area for trading and trapping. Nevertheless, Lisa persisted, though he had to deal in cash for goods and supplies. The expedition that left St. Louis in May of 1812 was small, carrying only about $11,000 worth of trade goods in two boats. It was not a good year for furs. Trapping had been poor during the winter when pelts were in their best condition, and the British predictably were attempting to stir up the Indians against the Americans. An attempt to open communication and possibly trade with the Spanish at Santa Fe came to nothing, particularly because of British-inspired Indian hostility in the intervening territory. The price of pelts in St. Louis was low because of the war, and the year showed less profit than hoped. Shareholders saw this as Lisa's fault and removed him from the board of directors of the company but continued to rely on him to run the trading expeditions.

The spring of 1813 found the citizens of St. Louis in a state of anxiety for fear of an Indian attack on the town. Nothing came of the alarm, but it contributed to a sense of unease and reluctance to invest in the future. Older inhabitants could remember with dread the events of 1780 when the British had sponsored an Indian assault of the city. Meanwhile to the north, Lisa was confronted by growing Indian anger and continued poor trading. In the summer of 1813, the directors decided to end the Missouri Fur Company and to sell its equipment and the relatively few pelts they had. Surprisingly, in December a vote for the formal dissolution of the company failed. Finally, in January of 1814, the directors forced through a motion to dissolve the company.

Lisa sought a new field of endeavor and found it in transporting goods from the United States Indian Factory, which produced trade goods, to Brownsville, Pennsylvania, located on the Monongahela River. Lisa set out with two boats but had to send one back as defective. In addition to transporting goods, Lisa sold buffalo robes at the various stops along the route. Transport might have occupied Lisa for the moment, but it was hardly a long-term solution to his ambitions.

In 1814, Theodore Hunt moved to St. Louis and purchased a lot and house from Lisa. Hunt and Lisa quickly formed a partnership with the intention of once again trading up the Missouri River. William Clark in his capacity as Indian agent appointed Lisa as agent to the tribes on the upper Missouri River and provided him with over $1,300 worth of merchandise to use to convince tribes to support the United States rather than Britain. Lisa set forth up the Missouri with both the government merchandise and that of the Hunt and Lisa partnership. Lisa made a vital alliance with the Omaha by marrying Mitain (also spelled Mitaine), a young woman from one of the important families according to Indian rites. Lisa's wife Polly was still alive but that seems not to have bothered Lisa. Taking Native wives was common at the time and advantageous to both parties. The trader gained guaranteed access to the tribes' pelts and skins, and the tribe gained guaranteed access to the trader's goods.

Portrait of Manuel Lisa, c. 1818, by an unknown artist. From *Journal of a Fur-Trading Expedition on the Upper Missouri, 1812-1813* by John C. Luttig, 1920.

Lisa's excellent reputation among the Indians enabled him to influence the Omaha, Oto, Teton, Yankton, Ponca, and most importantly the Sioux, which brought support for the Americans. Hostility between the tribes that supported the British and those allied with the United States, kept the British from effective use of the Indians against the Americans on the Missouri. August Pierre Chouteau did similar work with the Indians farther down on the lower river. By 1814, the war between Britain and the United States was ending, to be formally concluded in 1815. This did not mean a secession of hostilities among the tribes. They were slow to be moved to war, and even slower to return to peace.

In 1816, Hunt and Lisa's firm sent another expedition up the Missouri, despite competition from John Jacob Astor's much wealthier American Fur Company. Trading and trapping during the winter was good, in marked contrast to the last few years, and Lisa arrived back in St. Louis in June of 1817 with about $35,000 worth of pelts and skins. The partnership of Hunt and Lisa dissolved in 1818 according to a prior agreement, but the two remained friends and even cooperated for the 1818 trading and trapping season, during which Lisa ransomed a Spanish boy, about ten years old, from the Pawnees and brought him to St. Louis. There he saw to the boy's education and support.

In 1817, while Lisa was upcountry, his wife Polly died. While on the Missouri and before he knew of her death, Lisa attempted to gain custody of his two children by Mitain, Rosalie and Christopher. Mitain allowed Lisa to take Rosalie so she might be educated in a Catholic school, but she retained Chistopher. This may not have been to the boy's benefit. The Omaha was a strictly patriarchal society, so Chistopher was regarded as "white" because Lisa was his father, and so Christopher, though raised among the Omaha, had no place in the tribal structure. Lisa did not abandon his children by Mitain and made provisions for them in his will and for his children by Polly as well. Remarriage after only a short interval was common in the era, and in 1818 Lisa married a widow, Mary Hempstead Keeny, sister of a friend, Edward Hempstead. Lisa was at least nominally Catholic and Mary Keeny Presbyterian, so the pair were married by a Presbyterian clergyman. Lisa seems to have taken his Catholicism rather lightly. Also in 1818, Lisa had his portrait painted by a talented but unknown artist.

Lisa and many other leading merchants and traders formed a partnership for the 1819 trading season, which provided a rich assortment of merchandise and trade goods for him. Lisa as usual led the expedition. The partners, however, were not a trusting group, and frictions of various sorts caused problems from the start. Adding to the fray was the state of the economy in St. Louis at that time. Various banks had issued their own paper money, often without sufficient backing, and such notes were widely discounted with rates changing almost daily. A grave general economic panic also loomed, but beaver pelts brought good prices that year, and Lisa was able to form a new Missouri Fur Company with a more agreeable set of partners.

During the winter of 1819, Lisa fell ill. He returned to St. Louis in 1820, where his health rapidly declined. He made his final will on August 11, 1820, and died the next day. After a Solemn High Mass in the St. Louis Cathedral, Manuel Lisa was buried in the Hempstead burial plot, now part of the Bellefontaine Cemetery. Lisa's monument, now sadly eroded, still stands and may be seen today.

Manuel Lisa, throughout his life, was known for his fair dealing and respect for Indians, but far more than that he opened the upper Missouri River region to Americans. This became very important at the end of the War of 1812 when Britain and the United States were to define the northern border between Canada and the United States. George Rogers Clark's conquest of Vincennes and Lisa's forays and forts in the North practically defined the border settlement. Lisa's good reputation among the tribes and his work to ally Indians to the American cause effectively countered British efforts to employ Indians against the United States in the North. Lisa once spoke about his own personality, providing a brief sketch to which others would certainly have agreed: "I put into my operations great activity; I go a great distance while some are considering whether they will start today or tomorrow."[6]

6. W. Raymond Wood, *Lisa's Fur Trade Forts, and the Deaths of Potts and Drouillard*, https://lewis-clark.org/fur-trade/lisas-forts/; Hiram Martin Chittenden, *The American Fur Trade of the Far West*, 2 vols. (Stanford, California: Academic Reprints, 1954), 1:30.

INDEX

Abercromby, James, 71-72
Adams, John, 128
Albanel, Charles, 20
Algonquin, 3-4, 6, 10
American Fur Company, 151
Anglin, Ron, 133-134
Apache, 31, 40
Apekonit, 126-127, 129, 131
Arctic Ocean, 95-96, 99-100
Argenson, Pierre de Voyer, 13
Arikaras, 58, 144-145
Arkansas Post, 67
Arkansas River, 38, 40, 42-47
Assiniboine, 53-54, 56, 58-59, 144
Astor, John Jacob, 102, 147-148, 151
Aulneau, Jean-Pierre, 54
Avignon, 2
Avoch, 103

Baffin Island, 14
Bailey, Charles, 18, 20
Banque Royale, 30
Battle of Malplaquet, 51
Bay of Saint Bernard, 42
Beaubois, Nicolas-Ignace de, 32
Beauharnois, Charles de la Boische, 53-54, 58-59
Beaurain, Jean de, 39
Beautiful River, 58
Beaver tribe, 97
beavers, xiv, 8, 12-14, 22-23, 60, 135-138, 144-149, 152
Belgium, 70, 74
Bella Coola, 98, 101
Bellecourt, Joseph, 64-66
Benoit, Francisco Maria, 141-143
Beslot, Michel (La Rose), 64-66
Bienville, Jean-Baptiste Le Moyne, 32, 42, 46-47, 66
Bighorn River, 145
Bill of Rights, 120
Bissonette Antoine, 146
Black Hills, 58
Black Snake, 120
Blackfish, 116
Blackfoot, 136-137, 147-148
Blackwater River, 98, 101
Boisbriand, Pierre-Sidrac Dugue de, 31-32
Bonaparte, Napoleon, 141
Boone, Daniel, xiii, 106, 116-118
Boone, Nathan, 138
Bourgmont, Étienne de Veniard de, 25-34
Bourrie, Mark, 2, 5
Bowman, Joseph Lawrence, 76, 85-90

Bretagne Regiment, 51
Breton, Jeanne le, 37
Bridgar, John, 22-23
Bross, William, 111
Bruyere, Fabry de la, 66-67
Buade, Louis de, 20
Burnt Woods, 3
Burpee, Lawrence J., 50
Burr, Aaron, 106, 108-109
Butler, Simon, 114-115, 118

Caddo Nation, 39-40
Cadillac, Antoine Laumet de la Mothe, 26-27
Cahokia, 80, 82, 86-88, 141
Canada, 3, 5, 13, 16, 18, 22, 26-27, 49-50, 56, 65, 77-80, 92, 94, 99, 103-104, 153
Canadian River, 40, 67
Carr, Robert, 15
Carter, Harvey Lewis, 125, 128
Carteret, George, 15
Cartwright, George, 15
Carver, Jonathan, 94
"The Catt", 93
Cavelier, Rene-Robert (Sieur de La Salle), 40-41
Cedar Lake, 53
Cerisy, 25-26
Chaput, Donald, 80
Charles II, 15, 18, 20, 23
Chateau de Fountainebleau, 32
Chew, Polly C., 140, 150, 152
Cheyenne, 58
China, 52, 93-94, 99-100
Chippewa, 107
Chouart, Jean-Baptiste, 23
Chouart, Medard (Groseilliers), 2-3, 5, 8-18, 20-23
Chouteau, Auguste, 140-143, 145, 147-148, 151
Chouteau, Pierre, 140-143, 145, 147-148, 151
Churchill, John, 51
Churchill River, 93
Clark, George Rogers, xiii, 76-77, 80-90, 115-116, 118-119, 133-139, 143-145, 153
Clark, William, 142-143, 146, 149-150
Colbert, Jean-Baptiste, 22-23
Colter, John, 133-138, 146
Colter, Raymond, 140
"Colter's Run", 134, 136, 147
Comanche, 40, 67
Combe, William, 103
Committee of the Privy Council, 100
Compagnie des Indes, 28, 30, 32, 34, 39, 45-46
Compt, François Le, 144
Constitutional Convention, 120
Corps of Discovery, 135, 142-143
Couagne, Jean-Baptiste de, 69-72
Cree, 8, 12, 17-18, 23, 53, 94, 97
Curacao, 21

Dauphin Island, 30, 32, 53
David, Jean (Petit-Jean), 64-66
Dearborn, Henry, 129
Decker, Margriete, 109
Deerfield, French and Indian Raid, 50
Delassus, Charles Dehault, 141-142
Delaware, 82, 107, 109-110, 114-115, 126-127, 147
Delisle, Guillaume, 28-29
Dene Tha tribe, 94
DePeyster, Arent Schuyler, 81-82
Detroit, 26, 70, 81-83, 88, 90, 92, 118
Dickerson, Veach, 107
Dodson, Richard W., 121
Dollard, Adam, 12
Dowden, Martha, 120
Draper Manuscripts, 106-108, 121-122
Drennon, Jack, 115
Drouillard, George, 118, 137-138, 146, 148, 153
Drouillard, Pierre, 118-119
Ducoigne, Louis, 70
Dufresne, Marie-Michel, 74
Duke de Villars, 51
Dye, Eva Emery, 133-134

Eaglet, 17
Earl of Shaftesbury, 20
Edward, Duke of Kent, 103-104

Eel River, 126-127
English Channel, 16
English, William Hayden, 89
d'Estrees, Jean, 20-22

Fallen Timbers, battle of, 120, 128
Feast of the Dead, 11
Febvre, Joseph-Antoine le, 23
Fifth Voyage, 17
Finlay River, 98
Finlay, Gregory and Company, 92, 94
Finlay, John, 92
Flathead, 136
Fontenoy, 74
Fort Bourbon, 53
Fort Chartres, 3, 25, 70, 74-75
Fort Chipewyan, 94, 96-97, 101
Fort Clark, 81
Fort d'Orleans, 31, 33
Fort Dauphin, 53
Fort Dearborn, 130-131
Fort Edward, 70-71
Fort Fork, 97, 99, 101
Fort Harmar, 107
Fort Henry, 105, 148
Fort Kamanistikwia, 53, 55-56
Fort la Reine, 53, 56-59
Fort Lydius, 70-71
Fort Massiac, 74, 76, 86, 108
Fort Maurepas, 53-54, 56
Fort Orange, 4
Fort Pitt, 82
Fort Pontchartain de Detroit, 26
Fort Raymond, 135-137, 145, 148
Fort Rouge, 53, 56
Fort Saint Louis de los Cadodaquious, 39, 41
Fort St. Charles, 53-54, 56
Fort St. Pierre, 52-53, 56
Fort Wayne, 128-130
Fox, 32, 34, 52, 81
France, 20, 22, 30, 37, 40, 51, 56, 64-65, 71, 79, 86, 139, 141-142
Francome (Ensign), 42-43
Fraser River, 98
Frederick V, 16
French and Indian War, 74, 80, 110, 127, 139
French Marines, 26, 74, 80
French Rock, 43-45
French Service Hydographiqie, 58
French West Indies, 74
Fresne, Madelaine Tuvée Du, 63

Galien, Emanuel, 64, 66
Gallatin River, 137
George III, 103
Gibault, Pierre, 80
Gillam, Benjamin, 22-23
Gillam, Zachariah, 14, 17, 22-23
Girty, Simon, 115, 117
Godet, Charlotte, 24
Graham, Jane E., 72
Grand River, 31, 33
Grand-Menil, Jean-Vernon de, 3
Grand Portage, 53, 55, 93, 102
Great Slave Lake, 94-95, 97
Gregory, McLeod and Company, 92-93

Haldimand, Frederick, 81
Hamilton, Alexander, 108
Hamilton, Henry, 88
Hamtramck, Jean-Francois, 129
Harrison, William Henry, 122, 128-129
Harmar, Josiah, 107-108, 120
Harpe, Jean-Baptiste Benard, Sieur de la, 37-47
Harpe, Pierre, Seigneur de la, 37
Hayet, Marguerite, 3
Heald, Nathan, 130
Helm, Leonard, 81, 88
Hempstead, Edward, 152
Henry, Alexander, 94
Herrick Creek, 98
Hite, Jost, 85
Holland, 4-5
Horse People, 58
Hudson Bay Company, 1, 20, 22-24, 93, 100, 102
Hudson's Bay, 14-20, 22-24, 52-53
Hunt, Theodore, 150-151
Huron, 6-7, 10-11, 26

Hurtado, Jean Paez, 64-65

Incarnation, Marie de, 2, 5
Ireland, 17, 113, 133
Iroquois, 2-7, 9-15, 71-72, 106-107
Isenberg, Nancy, 108

Jackson Hole, 135
Jacob's Creek, 125
Jalack, 7
James VI, 16
James Bay, 14
James Creek, 98
James, James Alton, 89
Jarboe, Elizabeth, 121
Jefferson River, 136
Jefferson, Thomas, 81-83, 128-129, 142, 146
Jefferys, Charles, 57
Jemeraye, Christophe Dufrot, 52-54
Jesuits, 2, 4, 6, 8, 14, 16, 49
Johnson, William, 71
Johnston, John, 128-129
Jones, John Gabriel, 115
Jonquiere, Jacques-Pierre de Taffanel de la, 71
Journal Historique de l'Etablissement des Francais a la Louisiane (La Harpe), 46-47

Kanawa River, 114
Kaskaskia, 63-66, 69-70, 74-76, 81-82, 86-87, 140, 144, 148
Keeny, Mary Hempstead, 152
Kenton, Simon, 106, 113-123
Kentucky, map of, 117
Keweenaw Peninsula, 10, 12
Kickapoo, 81
King George's War, 71
King's Royal Regiment of New York, 92
Kiowa, 40
Kirke, Mary, 20, 23

La Gabelle (The Tax), 52
Labbadie, Sylvestre, 149
Labrador, 14
Lachine Rapids, 6
Laffont, Jean-Baptiste, 80
Lake Athabasca, 93-95, 101
Lake Huron, 10
Lake Michigan, 131
Lake Nipissing, 10
Lake of the Woods, 53-54, 56, 70
Lake Superior, 10, 53, 93
Lake Winnipeg, 53, 56
Lake Winnipegosis, 53
Langlade, Charles Michel de, 74, 80
Las Aves archipelago, 21
Law, John, 30
Lawrence, Thomas, 103
Leachman, William, 114
Legislative Assembly of Lower Canada, 77
Lenape (Delaware), 107, 110, 114-115, 126, 147
Lewis, Andrew, 115
Lewis, Meriwether, xiii, 118, 133-135, 137, 142-144, 153
Leyba, Fernando de, 76
Linctot, Daniel-Maurice Godefroy de, 79-83
Linctot, Hyacinthe, 79
Linctot, Maurice-Régis, 79
Linctot, René Godefroy, 80
Lisa, Christopher, 152
Lisa, Christoval de, 139
Lisa, Joaquin, 140
Lisa, Manuel, vii, 135-153
Lisa, Raymond, 140
Lisa, Rosalie, 152
Little Rock, 43-44
Little Turtle, 125-126, 128
Livingston, James, 120
Logan, Benjamin, 119
Logan's Station, 116-119
Lord Dunmore's War, 86, 106, 114-115, 134
Lord, Hugh, 74, 77
Louis XV, 32, 59
Louis XIV, 20, 23
Louisiana Historical Quarterly, 111
Louisiana Purchase, 142-143, 145
Louisville Literary News, 89

Luttig, John C., 151
Lydius, John Hendricks, 70-71

Mackenzie, Alexander, 91-104
Mackenzie, Geddes, 104
Mackenzie, Roderick, 93
Madame Montour, 27
Malgue, Louis-Hector Marin de La, 35
Mallet, Paul, 63-68
Mallet, Pierre Antoine, 63-68
Mandans, 50, 56, 58-59
Mantanne, 56-57
Marly, 32
Marquis de Seignelay, 22
Mascrier, Abbe Jean-Baptiste Le, 34-35, 46
Mason, George, 120
Matagorda Bay, 41-42
Maurepas, Jean-Frédéric Phélypeaux Count de, 53-54
McGillivray, William, 100
McGregor River, 98
McLeod, Normand, 92
McTavish, Simon, 100, 104
Memoires historique sur la Louisiane (Montigny), 34
Menard, Pierre, 144, 147-148
Mendoza, Domingo de, 65
Menominee, 10
Methodist Church, 123
Mexico City, 67
Miami, 26, 31, 81, 126-131
"Mississippi Bubble", 30
Mississippi River, 27-28, 30, 33, 40-42, 50, 63, 74-76, 81, 87, 120, 122, 139-141, 148
Missouri, Francoise, 32-35
Missouri Fur Company, 143, 146, 148-150, 152
Missouri Gazette, 139
Missouri River, 27-35, 56, 58-59, 75, 138, 143-153
Mitain, 150, 152
Mohawks, 3-4, 51
Monck, George, 15
Monongahela, 74, 150
Monroe, James, 146
Montgomery, Alexander, 119
Montigny, Jean-Francois-Benjamin Dumont de, 34-35, 44-46
Montreal, 3, 8, 12-13, 63, 70-72, 77, 79, 92, 100-103
Moogk, Peter N., 71
Moore, Arthur K., 111
Moreau, Louis, 64
Morgan, Louis M., 121
Morin, Louis, 64-65
Morris, Larry E., 133-134
Morrison, William, 144, 147-148
Murray, John, 114
Muskingum River, 107, 115, 127

Nasoni Indians, 40
Nassonite Post, 40
National Archives, 143
Nelson River, 17, 19
Netherlands, 20
New Amsterdam, 4, 15
New Chartres, 35
New France, 2, 5, 8, 14, 49, 51, 65, 71, 79
New Madrid, 122, 140
Newfoundland, 14, 51
Niagara, 72
Nolan, Charles, 56-57
Nonsuch, 17
Normandy, 25
North America, map of, 145
North West Company, 94, 99-100, 102-104
Notre-Dame Cathedral, 32
Nova Scotia, 16
Nuxalk, 98

O'Reilly, Alejandro, 140
Odawa (Ottawa tribe), 10, 26
Odell, George H., 39-40
Ohio Company of Associates, 127
Ohio River, 26, 72, 74, 76, 83, 86, 107, 115-122, 127-128
Ojibwe, 10, 12, 72
Omaha, 64, 150-152
Onondaga, 6-8

Osage, 31, 140-142
Osage River, 146
Oto, 28, 31, 151
Ottawa River, 10, 92, 107
Ouachipouennes, 53
Ouachita Mountains, 43
Ouaconisen, Ignon, 31-32
Ouiateanon, 81
Ozarks, 43

Padouca, 31
Painted Stone Station, 126
Parsnip River, 98, 101
Pawnee, 28, 58, 152
Peace River, 97-98, 101
People of the Bow, 58
People of the Glued Arrow, 58
People of the Serpent, 58
People of the Small Cherry, 58
Pensacola, 47
Peoria, 80-81
Pepys, Samuel, 17
Peru, 38
Piankeshaw, 81
Plague, 15
Platte River, 28, 144
Point Pleasant, battle of, 115
Ponca, 151
Pond, Peter, 94
Pope, William, 126
Port Royal, 16
Potawatomi, 10, 72, 81, 107, 130-131
Potomac River, 105
Potts, John, 136, 138, 147
Prairie du Rocher, 87
Praslin, Cesar Gabriel de Choiseul, 47
Prince Rupert, 16-18
Putnam, Rufus, 127

Quakers, 18
Quapaw, 43
Quebec, 3, 6, 20, 23, 25-26, 39, 77, 81
Queen Anne's War, 50
Queen Victoria, 103
Quick, Jacobus, 111
Quick, Tom, 109-112
Quick's Run, 119

Radisson, Pierre-Esprit, 1-24
Rainy Lake, 52-53, 56
Red Knives, 96
Red River, 37, 39-40, 53-56, 59, 64
Rees, 145
Reibaldo, Santiago, 65
Reminton, Frederick, 11
Ridaud, Pierre Francois de, 67
Rigaud, Philippe de, 26
Riu, Francisco, 74
Rivage, Gaston, 40
Riviere, Joseph Antoine Poncet de La, 4
Robitaille, Phillippe, 64-66
Rocheblave, Philippe-François de Rastel de, 73-78
Rockley Bay, 21
Rocky Mountains, xiii, 54, 101, 143-144
Rodriguez, Maria Ignacia, 139
Rokafull, Dona Maria de, 38
Roseborough Lake, 39
Rosencranz, Jacobus, 111
Rouensa, Elisabeth-Michel, 70
Royal Marines, 30
Royal Navy, 15, 17
Russia, 93

Sable, Louis Dandonneau du, 51
Sable, Marie-Ann du, 51
Saint-Denis, Don Louis de, 64
Saint-Malo, 2, 37-38, 48
Saint-Maurice River, 3, 14, 52
Sainte-Genevieve, 74
Salcedo, Manuel Juan de, 142
San Miguel de Linares de los Adaes, 40
Sanguinet, Carlos, 141
Santa Fe, 28, 43, 64-67, 143-144, 149
Sarpy, Gregorio, 141
Sauk, 81, 107
Sault Ste. Maries rapids, 10
Scotland, 16, 91, 104
Sekani, 98
Seneca, 72
Sergeant Dubois, 32, 34-35
Settlers Monument, 112

Seven Years War, 74, 139
Shannon, William, 81-82
Shawnee, 63, 69, 82, 114-122, 129, 131, 147-148
Sheppe, Walter, 92-93, 102-103
Shoshone, 58
Sikes, Philip, 108
Simcoe, John Graves, 99
Sioux, 8, 11-12, 52-54, 58, 149, 151
smallpox, 106, 111, 119
Smoke Hill River, 64
Smoky River, 97, 101
Snag Creek, 120
Spain, 15, 28, 30, 37-38, 40-41, 47, 51, 54, 64-67, 74-77, 80, 82, 93, 108, 118, 122, 139, 141, 143, 149, 152
spies, 16, 76, 115
Squire Boone's Station, 125
St. Clair, Arthur, 120, 126, 128
St. Deny, Charles Juchereau de, 26
St. Deny, Louis Juchereau de, 26
St. Joseph, 80
St. Lawrence River, 3, 92
St. Louis, 43, 63, 78, 83, 86, 118, 134-135, 137, 140, 142-143, 145-153
St. Louis Cathedral, 153
St. Philippe, 87
St. Pierre, 22
Ste. Anne, 22
Ste. Anne's Church, 70
Ste. Marie de Gannentaha, 6
Stuarts Draft, 133

Tecumseh, 122-123, 129-131
Tenskwatawa, 122, 129-130
Teton, 151
Thames, battle of, 123
Thompson, David, 94
Three Forks, 148
Tippecanoe, battle of, 122
Tisne, Claude-Charles du, 39
Tobago, 21
Todd, John, 119
Touret, Godefroy, 17
Treaty of Camp Charlotte, 115
Treaty of Greenville, 128
Treaty of San Ildefonso, 141
Trois-Rivières, 3-5, 13-14, 20, 23, 49, 52

United States Army, 127, 131
United States Indian Factory, 150

Vaudreuil, Louis-Philippe de Rigaud de, 82
Venezuela, 21
Vérendrye, Francois, 51, 58
Vérendrye, Jean-Baptiste, 51, 54
Vérendrye, Louis-Joseph, 52, 57, 59
Vérendrye, Pierre Gaultier de Varennes, 49-61
Versailles, 23, 32
Vincennes, 69-70, 76, 81, 88-90, 118, 140, 153
Vizarron, Juan Antonio, 65
Voyages from Montreal (Mackenzie), 102-103

Wabash River, 26, 81, 88, 107, 118, 120, 127-128, 140
War of 1812, 122, 138, 149, 153
War of the Austrian Succession, 74
War of the Quadruple Alliance, 40, 47
War of the Spanish Succession, 51
Ward, William, 122
Washington, George, 128-129
Wayne, Anthony, 120, 127-128, 131
Wea, 81, 126
Wells, Cary, 127
Wells, Samuel, 125-127
Wells, William, 125-131
Wetzel, John, 105
Wetzel, Lewis, 105-113
White River, 127
Wilkinson, James, 126, 147
Williams, Thomas, 115
Williston Lake, 98
Winnebago, 10, 52
Wichita, 40
Wivenhoe, 18
Wood, W. Raymond, 50, 153
Wyandot, 107, 114

XY Company, 102

Yankton, , 151
Yazoo River, 44
Yellow Creek Massacre, 106
Yellow Knives, 96
Yellowstone Lake, 135
Yellowstone River, 145
Yorktown, 119

Zautoouys, 43